# PHYSICAL EDUCATION ACTIVITIES
## FOR THE UNCOORDINATED STUDENT

# Physical Education Activities
## FOR THE
## UNCOORDINATED STUDENT

Susan J. Grosse
Monica C. Becherer

Parker Publishing Company, Inc.          West Nyack, N.Y.

**Library of Congress Cataloging in Publication Data**

Grosse, Susan J.
  Physical education activities for the uncoordinated
student.

  Includes bibliographies.
  1.  Physical education for handicapped children.
2.  Physical education for handicapped persons.
I.  Bercherer, Monica C.        joint author.
II.  Title.  [DNLM: 1.  Gymnastics.  2.  Sports.  QT255
G878p]
GV445.G76      790.19'6      74-23486
ISBN 0-13-667014-8

To Our Students:

*It's easy if you know how,*
*But it takes a lot of*
  *know-how to make it easy.*

  *Donald Boyle*

# WHAT THIS BOOK OFFERS

Every physical education class has at least one student (and more likely there are several) who cannot keep up with the group, who always seems to be falling over his own feet, who never gets picked for a team, and who generally speaking, just doesn't seem to fit into the class participation. It is an unhappy situation for both the student and the teacher. The student, discouraged by his inability to participate on the level of his peers, feels left out, inadequate, unhappy, and frustrated by his ineptness. These feelings may lead to complete refusal to participate, or to disruption of the class in an attempt to gain the attention he cannot receive in a normal fashion. Teachers may label him lazy, slow, clumsy, stupid, or troublemaker, but no matter what the name, the student has become a problem. He no longer receives any benefit from the class and he may be detracting from the activity of others. This book will help the teacher and the student deal with this situation and provide the ways in which it can be remedied.

The student just described has become a problem because basically speaking, he is uncoordinated, unable to control and manipulate his body with the degree of skill necessary for average class participation. It is this lack of coordination that is the concern of this book. The following pages contain a great variety of activities which will help the teacher give the uncoordinated student many different ways to discover how his body moves; to improve his control over this movement; and to help him develop the skill necessary for participation in activities on a level with others in his class. The key is variety—to meet the differing needs of the students as well as to provide materials for all areas of physical development, for coordination requires that all parts of the body's physical and mental systems function together. Hence, all areas of physical performance need attention.

7

The activities in this book can be used in several different class settings. Where those students with coordination problems have been separated from the regular physical education classes and placed in "adaptive" classes, these activities can become the focal point of the class period. Their maximum use will do much to improve those areas of functioning in which the students are deficient, and to speed the return of the student to the regular class. In situations where all levels of students must remain in one class these activities provide excellent warm-up situations for everyone, while giving particular attention to those students who show problems in the area of uncoordinated movement.

No matter what the setting, adaptive class or regular, it is possible for any physical educator to use these activities. In most cases they require little or no equipment. In several situations suggestions are made for making, rather than purchasing the needed items. A school's budget need not be a factor in the implementation of this program. Though a large gymnasium is nice, it is not always necessary, and the reader will also find activities that can be used in a relatively small space.

Perhaps the most important factor is the allowance made for progressive development. Once a program of coordination activities is begun, the teacher can select things to do based on increasing difficulty as well as variety. This enables the student not only to improve a particular weak area but also to integrate learned skills into his total functioning, gradually forming the hierarchy of activities needed for skilled participation. This progression can also be combined with the many self-testing factors which have been included, and thus, the student can become involved in setting goals for himself and in monitoring his own progress toward coordinated movement.

*Susan J. Grosse*
*Monica C. Becherer*

# CONTENTS

*9*

# *PHYSICAL EDUCATION ACTIVITIES*
## FOR THE <u>UNCOORDINATED STUDENT</u>

# 1

# RECOGNIZING THE UNCOORDINATED STUDENT

Coordination, a complex attribute of human movement, is the integration of neural and muscular processes which result in conscious control of purposeful movement. Many separate abilities contribute to its total development and as such, deficits in any of several different areas can result in a lack of coordination. The great variety of activities in which an individual may perform, each with a variable degree of coordination only tends to complicate the problem. Therefore, before giving our attention to the many activities which can be used to improve coordination it is necessary to take a brief look at coordination itself. It is only by knowing how coordination develops that one can accurately plan individualized programs of remediation.

Coordinated movement demonstrates control of balance, strength, and speed, and is executed with sufficient flexibility to ensure maximum efficiency in the use of time, space, and force. It is not just a matter of muscles. If it were, the problem would be simpler. However, the neural processes, which must work together with the muscular ones, are also very important.

Before initiating any movement, a person must have a reason to move. Perception, here, is the key, and its first stage is input. Something which happens in the environment is received by one or more of the sensory systems. The individual sees, feels, hears, touches, or tastes something. The nervous system transmits this information to the brain where several things happen. First, the incoming sensory information is evaluated and compared with past experiences stored in the memory. After the evaluation takes place, a decision is made relative to what reaction the individual will make in response to the input stimuli. Then the motor area of the brain takes over and sends out nerve impulses to the muscles causing them to initiate the appropriate motor activity, the movement output. After the motor activity has taken place, the sensory systems have more information to send to the brain regarding the results of the chosen course of action. This "feedback" comes from all of the sensory systems and is stored in the subsconscious for further use.

The movement output is made up of many different factors, the most important of which are balance, strength, flexibility, and speed. When the nerve impulses from the brain reach the muscle this muscle has to have reached a sufficient point in its development where it can respond with enough muscle fibers contracting to provide the amount of strength necessary to perform the desired movement.

Balance involves the ability to assume and maintain a body position in relationship to the forces of gravity, inertia, propulsion, and momentum. Though the sensory system for balance is in the labyrinth of the ear, it is the muscles of the body which are responsible for holding the various body parts in the desired position. The body must balance itself in static, mobile, and aerial situations, and in each case the properties which govern the movement of objects in space also govern the human body, and balance must be maintained in response to them.

Flexibility describes the range of motion which is possible in a joint. Though such range of motion is partially limited by the structure of the joint itself and the tissue that contains it, improvement can be attained by stretching the muscle fibers through use.

Speed falls into two general categories. One is reaction time—the time it takes for the individual to act upon the sensory input which he has received. It relates very closely to the degree of efficiency with which the brain processes sensory input information. Once the movement has been initiated, it must be maintained at some amount of speed. This is the second form of speed, and it is closely related to the strength of the muscle involved, combined with the body's metabolic capability for energy production. A muscle will continue to function at its peak only as long as its source of energy lasts.

The integration of these processes, if occurring adequately, will result in conscious control of purposeful movement. The person doing the moving will know what he is doing, or what he wants to do, and how he can obtain this goal. His body will be under his control in all aspects of voluntary movement. He will have a choice of where he wants to go and how he will get there, and he will do so in an organized way in relation to the rest of his environment. He will be coordinated.

## HOW DOES COORDINATION DEVELOP?

Coordination is dependent upon two basic factors: what a child is born with, in terms of his physical characteristics and mobility potential and what he does to develop what he has inherited. It is the breakdown in the development of these neural and/or muscular systems that can result in inadequate development of coordination.

Neurologically, a deficit can occur in many forms. The most common of these occurs when one of the sensory receptor systems is not functioning properly. An eye defect, for example, could cause a person to receive inaccurate information concerning the world around him. He might be unable to judge distance correctly or hit a target because he does not see it accurately. Unless such a defect is corrected the person will not be able to relate appropriately to what he sees and will be more likely to respond in an uncoordinated fashion. The same would be true if the deficit occurred in any of the other senses. The input would be distorted and as a result the person's actions would be impaired.

A less common neurological deficit can also occur when the brain itself is damaged. In such cases the damage could have occurred before or during birth, or be the result of an accident occurring at any time later in life. As brain tissue does not repair itself after an accident, any damage is of a permanent nature and its effect upon coordination is determined by the part of the brain which has been damaged. If the damage occurs in the motor area the usual result is cerebral palsy, a condition in which the brain sends out inaccurate stimuli to the various muscle groups. If the damage occurs in one of the higher brain centers it may affect the integration of information between the sensory and muscular systems. For instance, what is seen as being near may be interpreted by the brain as being far away, and the person may then walk into a table, even though his vision and his muscular system may be functioning perfectly. In such cases he has perceptual problems.

The neurological deficits cited above are generally of a physical nature. However, there are many cases in which another kind of neurological deficit occurs. In order for the brain to have information on which to base its judgments it must have some past experiences to draw upon. This experience begins when the child is born and continues throughout his life. An individual who does not have the usual variety of experiences in moving around in his environment when he is a child, or a person who has had inadequate or inappropriate experiences due to physical and/or mental deficits will not develop the background information needed to evaluate the more complicated movement situations encountered later in skill development classes. For example, most children play with a ball frequently during their childhood. However, if a child never sees a ball until he reaches high school it would be very difficult for him to play basketball with any degree of skill, or in fact, to even play a simple game of keep-away with his classmates who have been using balls all of their lives. This, of course, is an extreme situation, but the experiences of each child are different. Some students come into high school having had a great variety of physical experiences, while some have had almost none, especially in terms of formal skill development. It is this lack of experience which fails to provide the brain with the necessary information for dealing with more difficult movement problems.

Even if the neurological processes are functioning properly, uncoordination may still result if there has not been adequate development of the muscular system. Muscle strength can be improved by increasing the amount of strength the body must use to perform a desired task. Lifting heavier and heavier weights requires an increase in strength. Running while being immersed in water up to the shoulders requires more strength because the resistance is greater, and increasing the speed at which an exercise is performed also requires increased strength in order to maintain the muscular action. In each case, the improvement is progressive over time, restricted only by the maximum limits of the muscle.

Balance develops through a variety of experiences requiring balance in the three types of positions mentioned before: static, mobile, and aerial. In each case the person needs enough experiences to learn to feel the responses of his body to the various forces upon it, for it is only through an awareness of this feeling that the person is able to develop kinesthesis, and it is kinesthesis which provides vital information for keeping the body in balance during continuous motor activity.

Though the structural components of the joints of the body do limit their range of motion, a great deal can be done to make sure that the full range of potential motion is actually being used. If found to be insufficient for the demands of the activity, the range of motion can be increased through stretching activities. The ligaments surrounding the joint can be lengthened gradually, though it must be remembered that it is necessary to exercise the joint through its full range and not just confine the exercises to one or two planes.

Speed is partially dependent upon mental reaction and partially upon physical strength. If either is inadequate the speed of the individual will suffer. Reaction time can be trained through practice in responding to the desired stimulus. Muscle strength, as stated earlier, can be increased by increasing the resistance against which the muscle must work. It is when all of these factors are combined that skill learning really begins. Though each can be developed somewhat individually, they will eventually be used in various conbinations as the body works to perform purposeful movements. This is particularily true of students at the junior and senior high school level. As they begin to learn sports skills they draw heavily upon the neural and muscular capabilities that they have been developing as a child. If these areas have been developing normally the students have little trouble learning the needed skill through proper teaching and sufficient practice. However, there are a great many students who cannot put these factors together into skilled performance and it is these students who will be our concern in this text.

## IDENTIFICATION OF THE STUDENT
## WITH COORDINATION PROBLEMS

In many cases it is very easy to pick out the students who seem to be uncoordinated. A teacher can tell by the way they move, and the speed at which they learn or do not learn the skills being taught in class. However, there are many students who have coordination problems who are not identified in this manner because they have learned to cover up their inadequacy with other kinds of behavior, some desirable and some not. In order to help any student with coordination problems the person must first be identified.

There are two basic methods of identifying uncoordinated students. One is through teacher observation and the other is through formal testing. Teacher observation is perhaps the most commonly used, for it is the easiest, and usually, it is quite accurate when done within some guidelines. In addition to evaluating the degree of skill with which the child is performing, there are several other factors which a teacher should consider, including the student's behavior in class, his relationship to his peers, the emotional response that he has to the situation, and his capabilities in other subject areas. Though intensified observation on the part of the teacher may be concentrated in a few class periods, the teacher also needs to take a look at the frequency of the various behavior patterns which he observes. It may be necessary to make notes over a period of several weeks in order for the composite picture gained of the student to be accurate. Teachers should avoid making judgments about students based on only one or two observations.

The rating sheet, Fig. 1-1, can be used as a guide for the teacher in making his or her own evaluation, or it can be used specifically to identify those students who might have coordination problems. It is used by placing a check in the column which most accurately describes the frequency of the described behavior. The list is arranged so that if the student is substantially uncoordinated most of the even numbers will be checked always or almost always, and most of the odd numbers will be checked never or almost never. A scatter other than this might indicate problems in any of the five sub-areas listed.

Checklist for Identification of Uncoordinated Students

| Name: _____ Date: _____ | | | | | | |
|---|---|---|---|---|---|---|
| Behavior | | Frequency | | | | |
| | | Always | Almost Always | Sometimes | Almost Never | Never |
| Skill Development | 1. Learns new skills quickly. | | | | | |
| | 2. Trips or falls while performing. | | | | | |
| | 3. Follows verbal directions easily. | | | | | |
| | 4. Seems to perform quite slowly. | | | | | |
| | 5. Follows demonstrations easily. | | | | | |
| | 6. Has below average scores on fitness tests. | | | | | |
| | 7. Handles equipment with ease. | | | | | |
| | 8. Has excuses for not participating. | | | | | |
| | 9. Walks, runs, jumps easily. | | | | | |
| | 10. Looks uncomfortable while performing. | | | | | |

**Fig. 1-1**

|  |  | | | | | |
|---|---|---|---|---|---|---|
| Class Behavior | 11. Is attentive in class. | | | | | |
| | 12. Makes jokes about his own performance. | | | | | |
| | 13. Is used to demonstrate skills for others. | | | | | |
| | 14. Behavior is disturbing to the rest of the class. | | | | | |
| | 15. Uses practice time wisely. | | | | | |
| Peer Group Relationships | 16. Is usually one of the last people chosen for a team. | | | | | |
| | 17. Is chosen to be a leader or captain. | | | | | |
| | 18. Has few friends in class. | | | | | |
| | 19. Participates in intramural activities. | | | | | |
| | 20. Seems to withdraw from others. | | | | | |
| Emotional Outlook | 21. Enjoys sports. | | | | | |
| | 22. Gets discouraged easily. | | | | | |
| | 23. Responds readily to correction. | | | | | |
| | 24. Seems unsure of himself. | | | | | |
| Past Achievement | 25. Had previous high grades in physical education. | | | | | |
| | 26. Has good grades in most other subjects. | | | | | |
| | 27. Has good school attendance. | | | | | |
| | 28. Has poor grades in manual dexterity subjects. | | | | | |

**Fig. 1-1 *(Continued)***

After students who seem to have coordination problems have been identified through observation, a teacher may wish to further define the problems these students have by the use of formal tests. A survey of the literature on measurement in physical education would reveal a long list of tests to measure not only general coordination, but also several specific areas of coordinated skill development. If the teacher wishes to do formal testing, additional references may be found on the list at the conclusion of this chapter.

## WHAT ARE THE PROBLEMS OF THE UNCOORDINATED STUDENT?

As the identification checklist cited earlier may have illustrated, the uncoordinated student may exhibit quite a few problems for himself as well as for the teacher and the rest of the class. The most important of these, however, are the problems he poses for himself, as these are the ones affecting his behavior. In general they fall into three categories: his self-image, his relationships with his peers, and his physical development or lack of it.

By the time a student is in high school he knows how well he measures up to others of his own age group in terms of physical capability. The uncoordinated student knows that he doesn't perform very well and in a world which puts so much emphasis on physical capability, especially for its young men, to find one's self lacking can be quite a blow to one's self-esteem. Physical education is a class where everyone can see how well a student is doing, as opposed to perhaps an English class, where marks are on paper and can be hidden from classmates. When a student knows he is lacking in ability, he also knows that others can see his lack. This may result in either withdrawing from the class situation, through frequent absence or excuse, or the subsitition of other, more undesirable behavior, for the skills he does not have. In order for him to gain needed recognition he may be forced into an entirely different behavior pattern in compensation for his participation problems.

The uncoordinated student is not usually the most popular person in class, for who wants a poor player on their team or in their performance group? Though he may be a perfectly likeable person outside of class, he will not be accepted into a group which derives its status from athletic achievement. His place will be with others like himself, the group that is left out. For some students, those who have established interests and successes in other fields, this is not a great problem. They do not need to be accepted in an athletic world. But for some students, who have little success in any area, this may tend to isolate them further from acceptable peer group relationships.

A student who does not enjoy physical activity and does poorly in what he participates in is not likely to choose to participate when he does not have to. Nor is he likely to participate at his best when he is involved in activity. Therefore, his physical fitness and development is also likely to suffer. The body needs physical activity to maintain its healthy state. Inactivity results in poor organic functioning and eventually may precipitate a variety of health problems. This then becomes a vicious cycle, for the person who does not feel well does not usually want to participate in physical activity, thus completing the circle of nonparticipation.

The uncoordinated student is not going to be able to reach a very high level of physical functioning, nor is he likely to develop self-esteem or become involved in very many successful peer group relationships through physical activity. Though he may have other activities in his life to make up for this, it would be so much more beneficial for the student if the picture would be changed so that the uncoordinated student could change his own unhappy situation.

## CAN THE UNCOORDINATED STUDENT BE HELPED?

Overwhelmingly the answer is yes! However, the problems of the uncoordinated student are many and to him they may seem insurmountable. Therefore, the first step in the remediation process is a frank discussion of the problem with the student. He may hide his feelings about his poor performance under a mask of indifference or even dislike for any and every form of activity, but under this dislike lies a need to be accepted for successful performance with his peers. It is this desire to belong which the instructor can capitalize on. Once the student feels that he can improve himself, his attitude is very likely to change.

Together, the teacher and the student need to evaluate the student's present level of performance. The teacher has already done this to some extent in order to reach the conclusion that the student should be helped. Now the student needs to go through part of the the same process. The checklist used by the teacher can also be used by the student, and the two compared. The student can also evaluate his performance in the activities currently being done in class. Once he has determined his strong and weak points, a program of remediation can be considered.

The second step in the establishment of this program is obtaining a medical evaluation. In many situations the uncoordinated student has other health problems also—for example obesity, tendency to fatigue easily, or respiratory conditions, some of which may hinder his physical performance. In addition, due to the added stress that will be put on the body with an increase in activity it would be wise to determine if there would be any contraindications to strenuous activity. Figure 1-2 is intended as a sample form which may be sent to the student's private physician or used by the school doctor.

---

*Physician's Letter*

School Name
School Adress & Zip

Date _____

Dear Doctor _____,

   We are contacting you at this time regarding your recommendations for physical education activities for _____ *(student's name)*.

   The Physical Education program at our school is so planned that every pupil who is able to be in school should be able to derive benefit from some phase of this program. We have noted the following problems in his/her physical performance and would like to provide individualized activities to help this student to more active and enjoyable participation.

_____

_____

_____

(describe problem)

   Our classes run ___ minutes in length and meet ___ times per week.

   Please check (x) either generally or individually the type of Physical Education which you would recomend for this student.

| Mild ( ) | Moderate ( ) | Strenuous ( ) |
|---|---|---|
| ( ) Throwing—catch | ( ) Golf practice | ( ) Field Hockey |
| ( ) Throwing at target | ( ) Bowling | ( ) Softball |
| ( ) Table games | ( ) Softball, plastic | ( ) Tumbling |
| ( ) Billiards | ( ) Badminton | ( ) Volleyball |
| ( ) Shuffleboard | ( ) Folk and square | ( ) Apparatus |
| ( ) Bowling—plastic |     dance | ( ) Relay races |
|     equipment | ( ) Table tennis | ( ) Swimming |

**Fig. 1-2**

|  |  |  |
|---|---|---|
| *Mild* ( ) | *Moderate* ( ) | *Strenuous* ( ) |
| ( ) Softball—plastic equipment | ( ) Shooting baskets | ( ) Trampoline |
| ( ) Horseshoes | ( ) Creative movement remaining in place | ( ) Basketball |
| ( ) Bait casting | ( ) Archery | ( ) Cageball |
|  |  | ( ) Soccer |
|  |  | ( ) Golf |
|  |  | ( ) Jumping rope |
|  |  | ( ) Physical fitness activities |
|  |  | ( ) Track and Field |
|  |  | ( ) Weight lifting |
|  |  | ( ) Tackle football |
|  |  | ( ) Modern dance |

( ) No Physical Education permitted.

*Note:* If strenuous exercise is recommended, it is taken for granted that the mild and moderate activities are permissible unless exceptions are specifically stated; if moderate activities are recommended, again it is taken for granted that mild activities are permissible. Should you feel that generally the student should take only mild activity, but find that you feel one or two of the moderate activities such as bowling or golf should be included, simply check them.

Please feel free to ask any questions or make any additional comments that you feel may be of help to us and then please return this form to us as soon as possible.

Thank you for your cooperation.

Sincerely,

SCHOOL PRINCIPAL
PHYSICAL EDUCATION TEACHER

Comments: _____

_____

_____

Signed _____
Examining Physician

**Fig. 1-2** *(Continued)*

Once the medical recommendations have been obtained the next step is to set realistic goals for the future—physical feats to accomplish, as well as new types of activities to participate in, both in terms of what the student is capable of doing now and what he wants to be able to participate in during the future. Once these goals have been set the teacher and the student need to plan a program which will aid in progress toward these goals (Chapter 14). Obviously, the majority of activities will be chosen to improve those areas in which the student is weakest. However, because coordination means an integration of all areas of functioning, all of these areas should be eventually included in the program. Coordinated movement has many attributes and the activities chosen should benefit the development of as many of them as possible. Movement is considered to be coordinated if:

1. It is executed with the body in a relatively stable position in relation to the force of gravity. (It is balanced.)
2. It is performed easily enough to prevent undue strain on the body. (It has strength.)
3. It does not place the body in a position from which it cannot move effectively. (It shows flexibility.)
4. It is performed as part of the total flow of physical functioning. (It has rhythm.)
5. It is performed in a temporally efficient manner. (It is fast enough.)
6. It can be sustained sufficiently long enough to complete the purpose for which it was intended. (It has endurance.)
7. It serves the purpose intended. (It is skillful.)

Sometimes it may seem that a student is not capable of coordinated physical activity. This is especially true of those who are slow in learning other things, are retarded, have chronic health problems such as obesity, are brain damaged, or are physically handicapped. While they may never become varsity athletes these persons can still be helped to acceptable levels of performance in spite of their apparent difficulties. It is training that can make the difference. Just as the Olympic athlete needs special training to develop to his fullest potential, so does the student with movement problems. The average person never uses all of his capability—he never has to reach into his reserve of potential. But those with special problems need more help from others, and more effort from themselves, much in the same way the athlete does. They need to use every bit of ability that they do have and the proper activity program can help them to do this.

## FOR FURTHER REFERENCE

Brace, D. K., *Measuring Motor Ability*. New York, Barnes, 1927.

Drury, B. J., *Posture and Figure Control Through Physical Education*. Palo Alto, National, 1966.

Mathews, D. K., *Measurement in Physical Education*. Philadelphia, 1968.

Montoyne, H. J., ed., *An Introduction to Measurement in Physical Education*. Indianapolis, Phi Epsilon Kappa Fraternity, 1970.

Rushall, B. S., and D. Seidentop, *The Development and Control of Behavior in Sport and Physical Education*. Philadelphia, Lea & Febiger, 1972.

Safrit, M. J., *Evaluation in Physical Education*. Englewood Cliffs, New Jersey, Prentice-Hall, Inc., 1973.

Singer, R., *Motor Learning and Human Performance*. New York, Macmillan, 1968.

# 2

# SIXTY-ONE SIMPLE EXERCISES TO WARM UP

Bodily movement is executed by muscles and the only way that a muscle group can improve its functioning, and consequently improve the quality of this movement is through work. Though there are many forms of work that a muscle can do, the most basic of them is simple exercise, either isotonic or isometric. Isotonic refers to the fact that in addition to the muscle contraction itself some bodily movement also results, as opposed to isometrics where just muscle contraction is involved. There are some schools of thought which believe that greater muscle development will result from the isometric form since the contraction is performed at the muscle's maximum capacity. However, there are others who feel that the movement resulting from isotonic exercise greatly aids the performer in the later application of the muscle development. Both types of exercises are included here. It is up to the teacher to decide which type would most benefit the individual student and best fit the particular teaching situation.

Through exercise various areas of the body can be isolated and developed to whatever degree desired. Weak areas can be strengthened by fairly easy activities while stronger areas can be maintained at a high level of competency. The exercises described here are grouped according to the area of the body which they contribute to the most. Generally they fall into four subgroups: arms and shoulders; head and neck; legs and hips; and trunk. Within each group the exercises are listed progressively with the easiest to perform coming first. In addition, each exercise is coded according to what physical factor it is primarily responsible for developing: "Fl" for flexibility, or "St" for strength. Endurance in a muscle group can be improved by increasing the number of repetitions of a strengthening exercise. Balance is necessary in the performance of almost all of the exercises, since, for maximum benefit to occur, the parts of the body not directly involved in the exercise should be kept in the proper position of alignment. Generally, this position is stated at the beginning of the exercise description. Where there would be a tendency to lose this alignment special note is made in the exercise description. A "Glossary of Terms and Positions" is included at the end of the book to aid the reader in understanding these basic positions.

In deciding which exercises to use an important factor to consider is variety. The same few exercises every day would be boring for the student. Also, with only a few exercises, some parts of the body would very likely be neglected. Sometimes an unusual variation of an already familiar exercise can provide challenge and new interest to an "old hat" activity. There are many such variations included. As students become more proficient the number of repetitions can be increased, variations added, or different exercises substituted for familiar ones in the same category. This will help students to develop a background of exercises which will be of value to them in maintaining their exercise program outside of school and later on in adult life.

## ARMS AND SHOULDERS

*ARM CIRCLES*—(Fl) Straddle stand, arms extended sidewards at shoulder level and parallel to the ground, palms of the hands down facing the floor. Circle the arms forward in small circles, gradually increasing the size of the circle. When the arms are making as large a circle as they can, reverse the direction and gradually decrease the size of the circle until the starting position is reached. The arms should be kept straight during the entire exercise. See Fig. 2-1.
*Variation:*
1. Perform with the palms up facing the ceiling.
2. Perform from a starting position with the arms lifted in front of the body.
3. Perform from a starting position with the arms lifted directly overhead.
4. Have the arms circle in opposite directions during the entire exercise.
*SHOULDER CURLS*—(Fl) Standing position, arms hanging relaxed at sides. Curl the shoulders forward as far as possible without moving the rest of the trunk. Then press them backward, forcing the shoulder blades together, as far as possible. See Fig. 2-2. Repeat.

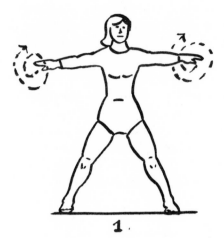
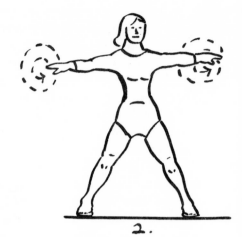

**Fig. 2-1**

**Fig. 2-2**

*Variation:*
1.  Raise both shoulders as high into the air as possible and then lower.
2.  Raise the shoulders up, then push them back. Lower the shoulders and then curl them foward, making a complete circle. Repeat in the opposite direction.
3.  Perform with the arms lifted to shoulder height and extended parallel to the floor.

*WING STRETCH*—(Fl) Standing position, arms flexed at the elbows and lifted to shoulder height with the forearms parallel to the floor. Fists slightly closed. Hands should almost touch in front of the body. Reach the arms across the front of the body to the opposite side, one arm over the other, keeping the

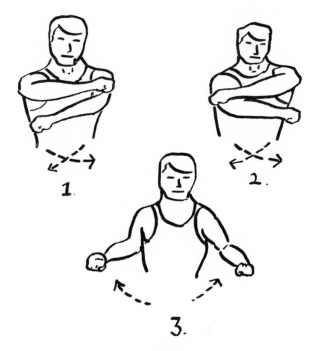

**Fig. 2-3**

elbows bent. Return to starting position. See Fig. 2-3. Reach across again as far as possible, letting the arm that went over the first time go under this time. Return to starting position. Now pull the elbows back as far as possible until the elbows point to the rear. Repeat. This exercise should be done fairly quickly.

*HAND PRESS*—(St) Standing position, elbows bent, palms of the hands flat against each other at chest level, fingertips pointing upward toward the ceiling. Press hands together as hard as possible and hold for ten seconds.
*Variation:*
1. Point the fingertips forward, away from the body.
2. Point the fingertips down and away from the body.
3. Do each of the hand positions with the arms completely extended in the same direction as the fingertips are pointing.

*ARM PULL*—(St) Standing position, elbows bent, fingers locked in an Indian grip, forearms parallel to the floor at shoulder height. Pull as hard as possible with both arms for ten seconds.
*Variation:*
1. Perform with the fingers locked behind the back of the neck.
2. Perform with the fingers locked behind the back at waist level.

*ELBOW PRESS*—(St) Back lying position, arms extended at shoulder level, elbows flexed so that the lower arms are off the floor and the hands are raised toward the ceiling. Press the elbows to the floor as hard as possible for ten seconds.

*PUSH-UPS*—(St) Front lying position, hands under the shoulders. Push up until the arms are straight. Lower the body back down to the floor. The ankles can be flexed and the balls of the feet placed on the floor to prevent slipping. The body should remain in alignment from the ankles to the head.

*Variation:*

1. Vary the width of the hand placement—less than shoulder width or greater than shoulder width.
2. Perform on the fingertips.
3. Flex the legs at the knee and allow the lower portion of the leg to remain on the floor.
4. Use only one arm. Keep the other off the floor.

*SHOULDER STRETCH*—(Fl) Kneel on both knees. Bend the trunk forward and extend both arms over the head placing the hands on the floor palms down. Try to push the body down from the shoulders. Bring the chest as close to the floor as possible. See Fig. 2-4.

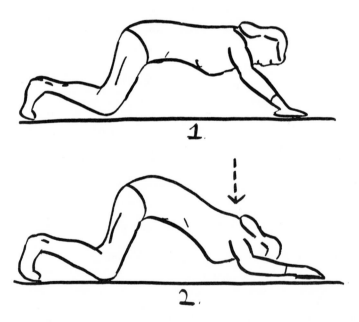

**Fig. 2-4**

*Variation:*

1. Perform with the arms folded in front of the body and supporting the head.
2. Perform with the hands placed on the floor under the chest as an aid to support.

## HEAD AND NECK

*FOREHEAD PRESS*—(St) Standing position. Interlace the fingers and place the hands on the forehead. Push the head forward while pressing back with the hands. Hold for ten seconds.

*HEAD PRESS*—(St) Standing position. Place the right hand on the right side of the head, just in front of the ear. Press the head and hand together as hard as possible and hold for ten seconds.

*NECK BENDS*—(Fl) Standing position. Turn the head first to the right, looking over the right shoulder, and then to the left. Keep the shoulders square and relaxed while moving the head. Perform slowly.

*Variation:*
1.  Tilt the head to the right and then to the left, bringing the ear as close to the shoulder as possible without lifting the shoulder.
2.  Bend the head forward bringing the chin close to the chest. Then tilt the head as far back as possible.
3.  Circle the head forward, tilt it to the left, tilt it back and tilt it to the right. Reverse the direction. Repeat.
4.  Assume a back lying position and curl the chin to the chest.

*NECK BRACE*—(St) Standing position, hands interlaced behind the neck. Push the head and neck backward, while pulling forward with the hands. Hold for ten seconds.

*NECK LIFTS*—(St) Front lying position with the arms stretched out in front of the body as far as possible. Lift the head and look at the ceiling and then lower. See Fig. 2-5.

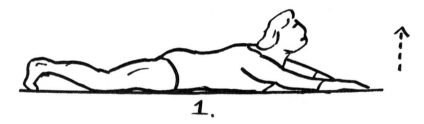

1.

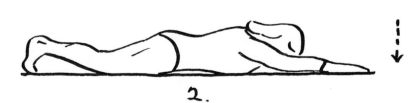

2.

Fig. 2-5

## LEGS AND HIPS

*ANKLE LIFTS*—(St) Standing position, heels together, toes apart, legs turned out at the hips, arms at the sides. Rise up on the balls of the feet and then lower the heels to the floor. Repeat.
*Variation:*
1.  Perform with the arms held parallel to the floor at shoulder height.
2.  Perform with the arms lifted directly overhead.
3.  Stand with feet turned out and shoulder width apart.
4.  Perform with the legs and feet in parallel position.
5.  Perform on one leg with the other foot held slightly off the floor.

*HALF SQUATS*—(St) Standing position, hands on the hips. Bend the knees and allow the heels to come off the floor. Lower the body half way down to the floor and return to a stand. See Fig. 2-6.

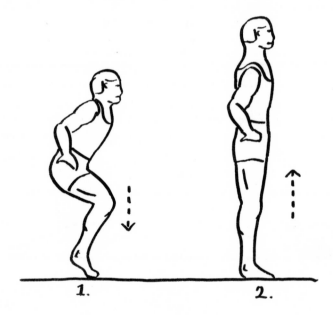

**Fig. 2-6**

*Variation:*
1.  Perform with the feet shoulder width apart.
2.  Half squat on only one leg. Extend the other leg straight out in front of the body.
3.  Perform from a forward/backward stride position.

*LEG BENDS*—(St) Standing position, heels together, toes apart, legs turned out at the hips. Keeping the heels flat on the floor bend the knees and lower the body as far as possible. Straighten the legs and return to a stand. Perform slowly.

*Variation:*
1. Perform from a side-stride straddle stand position.

*BOBBING*—(Fl) Standing position. Bend the trunk forward touching the floor with the hands. Keep the legs straight. Do not bend the knees nor hyperextend the knees. Bob to the floor three times and then return to a standing position. See Fig. 2-7.

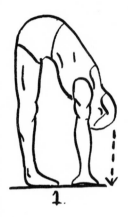

**Fig. 2-7**

*Variation:*
1. Perform from a straddle stand position.
2. On the three bobs touch first the fingers, then the palms, and then the elbows to the floor.
3. Stand with the legs in a forward/backward stride position. Bob over the forward leg.
4. Clasp the hands behind the back and bob, getting the head as low as possible.

*THIGH STRETCH*—(Fl) Standing position. Raise one leg, lifting the foot off the ground behind the body. Reach back and grasp the raised leg at the ankle. Pull the foot toward the buttocks and then allow the thigh to return forward. See Fig. 2-8. Repeat with the other leg.

*LUNGE*—(Fl) Stand in a forward/backward stride position. Turn the back foot and leg outward. Shift the weight forward over the front foot. Bounce forward slightly. See Fig. 2-9.

*Variation:*
1. Perform with the feet in parallel position. The weight will not be as far forward, and the bounce will be more up and down.

*HIP STRETCHER*—(Fl) Stand in a wide straddle stand position, with the toes apart and the heels together, legs turned out at the hips. Keeping the body

**Fig. 2-8**

**Fig. 2-9**

erect lower it by bending at the knees. When the body is as low as possible bob gently. Be sure to keep the knees over the toes and the body erect.

*FLUTTER KICKS*—(St) Front lying position, arms at sides. Raise the legs off the floor. Raise the head. Move the legs alternately in an up and down fashion as in swimming. See Fig. 2-10.

*Variation:*

1. Perform from a back lying position.
2. Instead of moving the legs up and down, when they are lifted off the floor have them alternately cross and then stretch far apart.

**Fig. 2-10**

*SIDE LEG RAISES*—(Fl) Side lying position, one arm on the floor extended under the head and the other, top arm, bent with the hand placed on the floor in front of the body for support. Keeping both legs straight, lift the top leg as high toward the perpendicular as possible. Lower slowly back to the other leg. See Fig. 2-11. Repeat. Change to the other side and perform with the other leg.

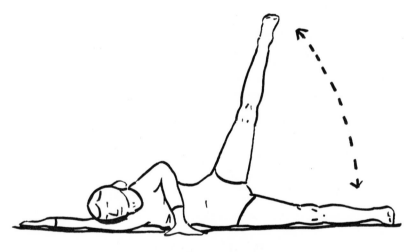

**Fig. 2-11**

*LEG LIFTS*—(Fl) Back lying position, arms on the floor perpendicular to the body at shoulder level. Keeping the shoulders and the inactive leg on the floor, lift the other leg till it forms a 90° angle with the floor. Then lower it to the side and try to touch the foot to the opposite hand. Return to the perpendicular and lower the leg to the floor. See Fig. 2-12. Repeat using the other leg.
*Variation:*
1. Lift both legs together and lower to the same side.
2. Lift one leg to the perpendicular and then lower it sidewards to the same

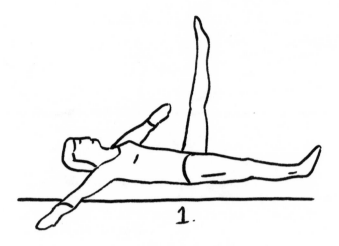

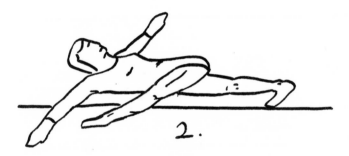

**Fig. 2-12**

side, (right leg to right hand). Return to the starting position by sliding the
foot along the floor.

*BICYCLE*—(St) Back lying position. Lift the legs and hips to a shoulder stand.
Support the hips with the hands. Move the feet and legs as if riding an
imaginary bicycle. See Fig. 2-13.

*Variation:*

1. Lower the legs to a pike position and peddle.
2. Instead of lifting the legs to a shoulder stand lift them only 45° off the
   floor.
3. Bicycle in a reverse direction.
4. Vary the speed of the leg action.

*THIGH BOUNCE*—(Fl) Hurdle sitting position. Lower the trunk backward to the
floor. Bounce the thigh of the bent leg lightly. Try to get it to touch the floor.
See Fig. 2-14. Repeat with the other leg.

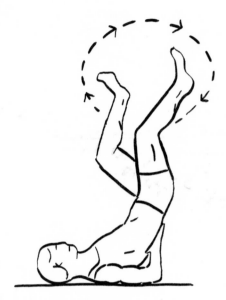

**Fig. 2-13**

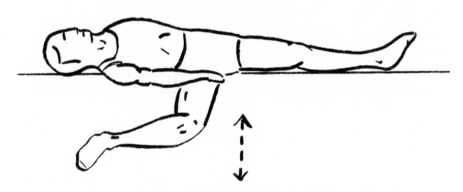

**Fig. 2-14**

*HURDLER'S EXERCISE*—(Fl) Hurdle sitting position. Bend forward over the straight leg, reaching for the foot of the extended leg with the hands. See Fig. 2-15. Repeat with the other leg extended.

*Variation:*

1.   Reverse the bent foot position. Tuck the foot in next to the thigh.

2.   Place the foot on top of the thigh.

*BODY BEND*—(St) Kneel on both knees with the body erect, arms hanging at the sides. Lean backward until the angle of the body with the floor reaches 45° and then return to an upright position. Do not let the trunk bend. See Fig. 2-16.

**Fig. 2-15**

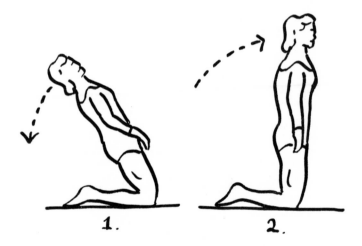

**Fig. 2-16**

*Variation:*
1.   Perform with the arms extended directly overhead.
2.   Perform with the arms raised to shoulder level and parallel to the floor.

*SPRINTER*—(St) Assume a push-up position. Bend one leg and place the ball of
   that foot on the floor even with the knee of the other leg. Spring slightly into
   the air and while off the ground exchange leg positions so that the extended
   leg is flexed and the flexed leg is extended on landing. Repeat, exchange legs
   again and land.

*SKI KICK*—(St) Push-up position. Bend one knee and bring it as close to the
   chest as possible. Then kick the leg straight back with a quick action. See Fig.
   2-17. Repeat with the other leg.

*POP-UP*—(St) Standing position, arms at the sides. Jump high into the air. Tuck
   the legs up and close to the chest, grasping them with the arms at the height of
   the jump. Land in the starting position. See Fig. 2-18.

Fig. 2-17

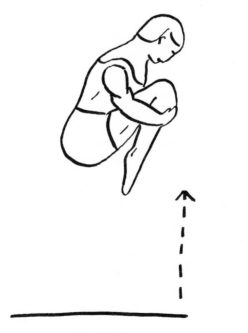

Fig. 2-18

*SPLIT JUMP*—(St) Standing position with the knees bent slightly and the hands on the hips. Place one foot forward into a forward/backward stride. Jump upward and while in the air change the foot positions and land with the other foot forward. Be sure to keep the body erect. See Fig. 2-19.

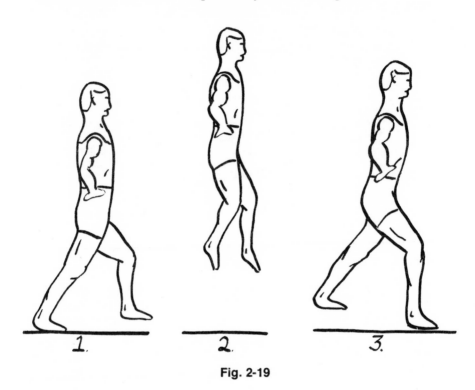

**Fig. 2-19**

*Variation:*
1. Jump from a lunge position.
2. Perform from a wide forward/backward stride.

*JUMPING JACK*—(St) Standing position, arms at the side. Jump to a side-stride position and lift the arms overhead. Jump back to the starting position.
*Variation:*
1. Jump into a forward/backward stride position.
2. Alternate jumping side-stride and forward/backward stride.

*KANGAROO LEAP*—(St) Standing position. Jump off from both feet. In the air extend the arms out sideward, lift the head and chest, and arch the back as much as possible. Land in the original position. See Fig. 2-20.

*HEEL STRETCH*—(Fl) Stand with the feet together, the trunk bent forward until the hands can be placed on the knees. While keeping the heels flat on the floor bend the knees as far as possible. Bounce two counts. Then rise back to the original position and press back on the knees two counts. See Fig. 2-21. Repeat.

**Fig. 2-20**

**Fig. 2-21**

*JUMP TURN*—(St) Standing position. Jump into the air off both feet. While in the air twist the body and make a full turn. Land in balance on the same spot the take-off was made from.

*SPLITS*—(Fl) Take a forward/backward stride position. Place the hands on the floor in front of the trunk. Allow the rear leg to slide out as far back as possible, taking some weight on the hands if necessary. Bounce lightly when the body is as far down as possible. Repeat with the other leg backward.

*CHINESE SPLITS*–(Fl) Wide side-stride position. Bend forward at the waist. Place the hands on the floor to add to the body support. Allow the legs to slide as far as possible out to the sides. When the body is as low as possible bounce gently. See Fig. 2-22.

*Variation:*

1. From the lowest position place one hand forward and one hand backward and rock back and forth.

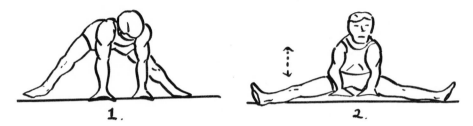

**Fig. 2-22**

## TRUNK

*ABDOMINAL PULL*—(St) Standing position. Tighten the abdominal muscles and pull in the stomach as far as possible. Hold for ten seconds.

*STOMACH TIGHTENER*—(St) Standing position, arms at the sides. Pull in the abdominal muscles as hard as possible and release. Perform this tightening and relaxing as quickly as possible.

*BODY BEND*—(Fl) Straddle stand position with the arms parallel to the floor, shoulder level high. Lean laterally to one side, sliding the arm on that side down the leg and reaching overhead with the other arm. Bounce, reaching as far as possible. See Fig. 2-23. Repeat to the other side.

**Fig. 2-23**

*Variation:*
1.   Perform from a forward/backward stride position.

*STRADDLE STRETCH*—(Fl) Sit in the straddle position, with the hands on the
hips. Bend the trunk forward from the waist and bounce, trying to touch the
forehead to the floor. The toes are pointed. See Fig. 2-24.

STARTING POSITION

**Fig. 2-24**

*Variation:*
1.   Bend the body first over one leg and then over the other in the bounces.
2.   Vary the arm position by lifting the arms overhead, holding them parallel
     to the floor at shoulder level or reaching forward toward the toes.
3.   Flex the ankles and point the toes toward the ceiling.

*TRUNK CIRCLES*—(Fl) Straddle standing position, hands on the hips. Circle the
trunk by flexing at the waist, leaning first forward, then left, backward and
then right. See Fig. 2-25. Reverse the circle, and repeat.
*Variation:*
1.   Perform with the feet together.
2.   Perform with the legs in a forward/backward stride position.

*WINDMILL*—(Fl) Straddle standing position, with the arms extended at shoulder
level and parallel to the floor. Bend the body forward. Twist from the waist
and at the same time reach with the one hand for the toe of the opposite foot.
Look back over the shoulder in the direction in which you are twisting and
focus on the high hand. Keep both arms straight. See Fig. 2-26. Repeat to the
other side.

*TRUNK TWIST*—(Fl) Straddle standing position with the arms apart, parallel to
the floor at shoulder height. Twist from the waist side to side. See Fig. 2-27.
*Variation:*
1.   Perform from a forward/backward stride position.

Fig. 2-25

Fig. 2-26

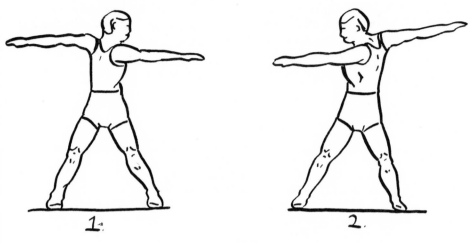

**Fig. 2-27**

2. Perform from a normal standing position.
3. Relax the arms at the sides and allow them to swing freely during the twist.
4. Flex the arms at the elbow with the fists almost touching in front of the body. Twist forcefully.

*BOUNCES*—(Fl) Long sitting position. Reach forward with both arms and bounce forward trying to touch the forehead to the knees. The arms may be used to pull forward by grasping the ankles. The toes should be pointed. See Fig. 2-28.

**Fig. 2-28**

*Variation:*
1. Perform with a variety of arm positions: hands behind the neck, arms extended parallel to the floor at shoulder level, or directly overhead.
2. Perform with the ankles flexed and the toes pointed toward the ceiling.

*LITTLE BOUNCES*—(Fl) Sit on the floor with the knees bent and the soles of the feet flat against each other. Grasp the feet and pull the trunk over the feet and close to the floor. Bounce forward lightly from this position. See Fig. 2-29.

**Fig. 2-29**

*KNEES TO SHOULDERS*—(Fl) Back lying position with the arms at the sides, knees bent, feet flat on the floor. Pull both knees up to the chest. Grasp the knees with the arms and pull in tightly. Tuck the head forward and rock back and forth. See Fig. 2-30.

**Fig. 2-30**

*Variation:*
1. Perform with the legs straight.
2. Rock from side to side instead of back and forth.

*SITTING ARM SWING*—(Fl) Long sitting position with the arms straight at the sides, raised to shoulder level and parallel to the floor. Keeping the seat on the floor, twist the trunk as far as possible to the right and then to the left. See Fig. 2-31.

**Fig. 2-31**

*Variation:*
1. Perform with a variety of arm positions. Try directly overhead, parallel to the floor, in front of the body, or with the elbows bent so that the arms encircle the body on the twist.

*TUCK TWIST*—(Fl) Back lying position. Lift the legs and bring the knees to the chest. Keeping the shoulders on the floor, twist the trunk and touch the knees to the floor on the right side of the body. Return to center and then twist the knees to touch on the left side. See Fig. 2-32. Repeat.

*WAIST TWIST*—(Fl) Straddle sitting position. Keeping the hips on the floor, reach behind and close to the body with both hands going to the same side. Dip the body down as close to the floor as possible. Take the weight on the arms and attempt to touch the chest to the floor. See Fig. 2-33. Switch hands to the other side and repeat.

*ABDOMINAL STRETCH*—(Fl) Front lying position with the hands on the floor next to the shoulders. Push up on the arms, straightening the elbows and

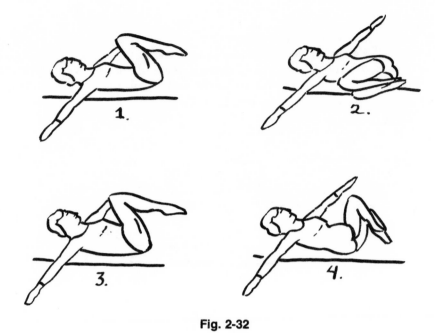

Fig. 2-32

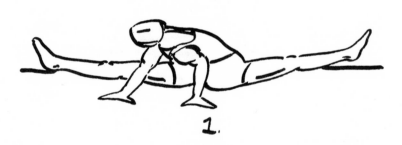

Fig. 2-33

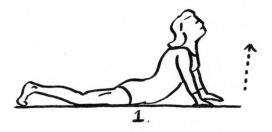

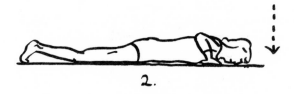

**Fig. 2-34**

arching the back. Keep the hips on the floor. Return to the front lying position. Perform quickly. See Fig. 2-34.

*PRONE LEG LIFT*—(St) Front lying position, the arms at the sides near the hips with the palms down. The forehead is on the floor. Lift the legs and hips off the floor as high as possible. Keep the legs straight. Lower to the floor. See Fig. 2-35. Repeat.

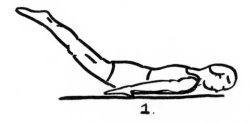

**Fig. 2-35**

*ROCKER*—(Fl) Front lying position. Reach back and grasp the feet with the hands. Arch the body, lifting the legs and chest off the floor. See Fig. 2-36. Return to the starting position and repeat.
*Variation:*
1.  Rock back and forth in the arched position.
2.  Extend the arms over the head. Raise arms, trunk, and legs and rock back and forth.

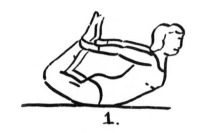

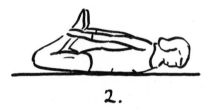

**Fig. 2-36**

*DOUBLE LEG LIFT*—(St) Back lying position. Keeping the legs straight, lift them both until the toes are pointed toward the ceiling. Lower back to the floor. See Fig. 2-37.
*Variation:*
1.  Lift the legs and then lower very slowly taking ten seconds to reach the floor.
2.  Lift the legs to a 90° angle. Keeping the hips on the floor, lean the legs to the right as far as possible. Return to center and lower to the floor. Repeat leaning on the other side.

*BODY CURL*—(St) Long sitting position. Lower the trunk to the floor backward. Lift the legs and hips overhead until the toes touch the floor behind the head. The legs should remain straight. Lower the legs and return to the long sit position. See Fig. 2-38.
*Variation:*
1.  Pause momentarily with the legs overhead in a shoulder stand and lower only one leg to the floor behind the head. Return that leg to the shoulder stand and then lower the other leg.
2.  Perform with the legs in a straddle position.

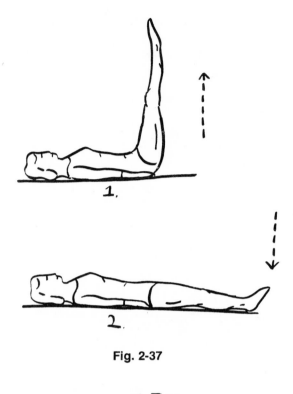

**Fig. 2-37**

**Fig. 2-38**

3.  Bend the knees and bring the legs in as close to the shoulders as possible while in the curl position.
4.  Walk in small steps first to one side and then to the other while in the curl position.

*REVERSE PUSH-UP*—(St) Back lying position with the knees bent and the feet flat on the floor close to the hips. Place the hands on the floor next to the shoulders, with the fingers pointing toward the shoulders. Push up with the arms and legs, lifting the body off the floor as high as possible. Return to the floor and repeat. See Fig. 2-39.

1.

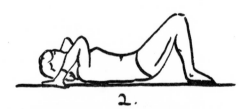

2.

Fig. 2-39

*SHOULDER STAND*—(St) Back lying position. Lift the legs and hips until the toes are pointed straight for the ceiling. The arms and hands may be used to support the hips. Keeping the legs straight hold this position for ten seconds and then lower to the floor. See Fig. 2-40.
*Variation:*
1.  Vary the arm position. Place the arms overhead, straight at the sides or extended at shoulder level.
2.  Vary the leg position in the air. Try a pike, straddle, scissors, or tailor position.

*TRUNK LIFT*—(St) Front lying position. Bend the arms and place the hands behind the neck. Lift the upper body off the floor as high as possible. Hold for ten seconds and return to the floor. See Fig. 2-41.

**Fig. 2-40**

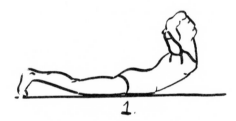

**Fig. 2-41**

*Variation:*
1. Vary the arm position. Try holding them parallel to the floor at shoulder level or lay them next to the sides of the body.

*V SEAT*—(St) Long sitting position. Place the hands at the sides next to the hips. Lift the legs off the floor as high as possible and hold for ten seconds. Keep the legs straight, and the trunk straight from the hips to the head.

*Variation:*
1. Grasp the raised legs with the hands and pull them to the chest.
2. Vary the arm position. Try them raised straight overhead, or parallel to the floor at shoulder level.

3.  Start from a back lying position and lift the legs and trunk at the same time.
4.  Do not hold for ten seconds but rather perform in quick repetitions.

*SIT-UPS*—(St) Back lying position, knees bent, with the feet flat on the floor and the arms at the sides. Lift the trunk up bringing the body as close to the knees as possible. Return to the starting position.

*Variation:*
1.  Vary the arm position by placing the arms behind the head, extended over the head or crossed over the chest.
2.  Perform with the legs straight.
3.  Vary the speed of the exercise.
4.  Sit up with a body twist, touching the right shoulder to the left knee and then the left shoulder to the right knee.

## FOR FURTHER REFERENCE

Consult the listing at the conclusion of Chapter 3.

# 3

# EXERCISE COMBINATIONS
# TO ADD CHALLENGE

Once individual body areas have been improved through simple exercises, the next step toward coordinated movement is the combination of the various physical factors already described. The arms, legs and trunk need to be able to work together performing a variety of different and sometimes opposing actions. This requires the interaction of balance, strength, flexibility and endurance. The exercises in this chapter provide for this integration without demanding a great deal of sport skill, as would participation in games. They are composed of many of the same movements learned in the simple exercises from the preceding chapter, but the way in which these movements are put together increases the difficulty of the exercise and demands more coordinated performance from the student.

These combinations are grouped into four categories. The first set of combinations involve those done in a stationary position. The weight of the body will remain on a relatively stable base and only one or two body parts will be involved in the exercise. The second group are those combinations which demand a change of the level of the body, ranging from high and erect through medium, or slightly bent, to low, flat on the floor. The third are changes of direction. These involve exercises which require an alternation between the sides of the body, and help a student to overcome the one-sidedness of many uncoordinated performers. Moving through space constitutes the last category. This movement may be just leaving the ground in one place as in a jump or hop, or it may be an intricate trip across the floor performing a variety of locomotor patterns. Within each group the exercises are arranged progressively in order of difficulty, with the easiest first.

Activities should be chosen from all four groupings. Each has its own special value and makes a different contribution to the development of coordination. Remember that a variety of exercises will keep the student from becoming bored and the adding of new exercises every day will provide challenge by increasing the difficulty.

The descriptions are arranged according to the counting done in the performance of the combination. Many of them have several parts and it is necessary to provide some order to the activity. Though the speed of the exercise can be varied, the counting should be even. If one segment of the exercise takes longer than another more counts are alotted to it. Maintaining the counting will also help the performer to establish rhythm and provide some continuity to his actions.

## STATIONARY POSITIONS

*ARM RAISES*—Standing position, arms at the sides.
1. Lift the arms forward in front of the body until they are parallel to the floor.
2. Extend the arms directly overhead.
3. Open the arms out and lower them to a sideward position level with the shoulders.
4. Lower the arms to the side. See Fig. 3-1.

1.          2.          3.          4.

**Fig. 3-1**

**BODY ARCHES**—Straddle standing position, arms at the sides.

   1. & 2.     Swing the arms forward and up overhead while arching the back and tilting the head backward.

   3. & 4.     Swing the arms forward and down while bending the body forward from the waist, allowing the arms to swing upward behind the back. See Fig. 3-2.

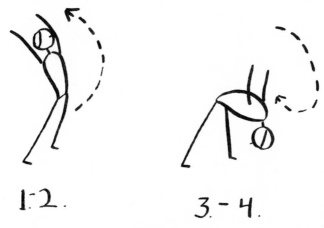

**Fig. 3-2**

**FIGURE EIGHT**—Standing position, arms at the sides.

   1.  Keeping the arms straight, reach behind the body and move them so that the fingers trace a figure eight pattern in the air.

   2.  Swing the arms forward and trace a figure eight pattern in the air in front of the body. See Fig. 3-3.

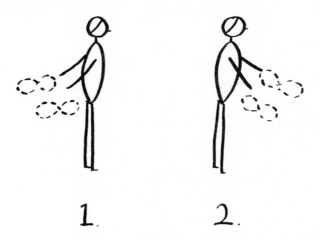

**Fig. 3-3**

*PENDULUM SWING*—Straddle standing position, arms at the sides.
> 1. & 2.    Swing the arms up as high overhead as possible.
> 3. & 4.    Swing the arms down and back behind the body as far as possible. See Fig. 3-4.

**Fig. 3-4**

*ARM CIRCLES*—Standing position, arms at the sides.
> 1.         Raise the arms sideward till they are parallel with the shoulders.
> 2.         Touch the hands to the tops of the shoulders.
> 3.         Raise the arms directly overhead.
> 4.         Touch the hands to the shoulders.
> 5.         Extend the arms at shoulder level.
> 6, 7, 8.  Move both arms in opposing circles, starting downward and crossing in front of the body, and finish with them next to the sides. See Fig. 3-5.

*ARMS UP*—Standing position, arms at the sides.
1. Swing the arms backward in a circular motion until they are directly over head.
2. Pull the hands straight downward somewhat forcefully by sharply bending the elbows.
3. Thrust the arms back upward into extension.
4. Swing the arms forward and down to their original position at the sides. See Fig. 3-6.

*DOUBLE LEG LIFTS*—Back lying position, arms at the sides.
1. Lift the legs and hips into a shoulder stand.
2. Lower the legs into a pike position while balanced on the shoulders.
3. Return to a shoulder stand.
4. Lower the legs and hips to the floor. See Fig. 3-7.

The hands may be used to support the hips in the shoulder stand.

Fig. 3-5

Fig. 3-6

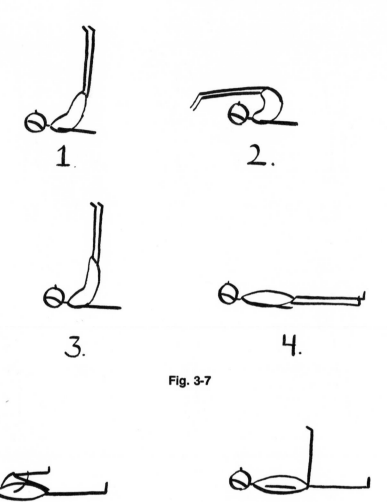

**1.**

**2.**

**3.**

**4.**

Fig. 3-7

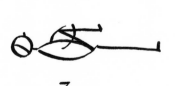

**1.**

**2.**

**3.**

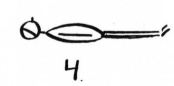

**4.**

Fig. 3-8

*HAMSTRING STRETCH*—Back lying position, arms at the sides.
1.   Flex the right leg at the knee and grasping the knee with both hands pull it to the chest.
2.   Extend the right leg upwards, perpendicular to the floor.
3.   Grasp the right knee and pull it back to the chest.
4.   Extend the leg on the floor. See Fig. 3-8. Repeat with the other leg.

*LEG LIFTS*—Standing position, arms at the sides.
1.   Simultaneously lift the right leg and left arm sideward as high as possible and lower back to position.
2.   Lift the right leg forward and left arm backward as high as possible, and lower.
3.   Lift the right leg and left arm sideward as high as possible and lower.
4.   Lift the right leg backward and the left arm forward as high as possible and lower. See Fig. 3-9.

Repeat with the opposite arm and leg action.

**Fig. 3-9**

*LEG KICKS*—Back lying position, arms at the sides.
  1. Lift both legs together to a 90° angle with the floor.
  2. Open the legs in a split position sideward.
  3. Bring the legs together.
  4. Flutterkick four times as the legs are slowly lowered to the floor. See Fig. 3-10.
The legs should be kept straight during the entire exercise.

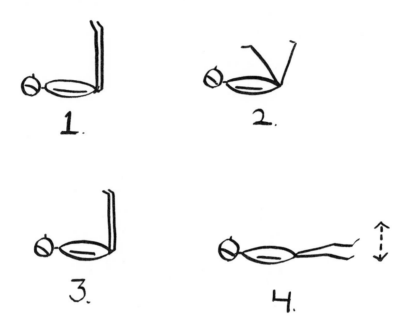

**Fig. 3-10**

*BACK FLEXIONS*—Back lying position, arms at the sides, palms on the floor, toes pointed.
  1. Flex the ankles so that the feet are at a 90° angle to the floor. Then extend the ankles pointing the toes. Repeat the flexion and extension three more times.
  2. Continue part 1 and add flexion of the wrist to a 90° angle with the floor and then extension placing the palms back down on the floor. Repeat these two together three more times. See Fig. 3-11.
  3. Continue parts 1 and 2 and add a flexion of the neck, touching the chin to the chest and then lowering the head back to the floor. Repeat these three together three more times.
  4. Continue parts 1, 2, and 3 and add a curl of the shoulders and chest, lifting the shoulders off the floor as far as possible and then returning to the floor. Repeat these four three more times.

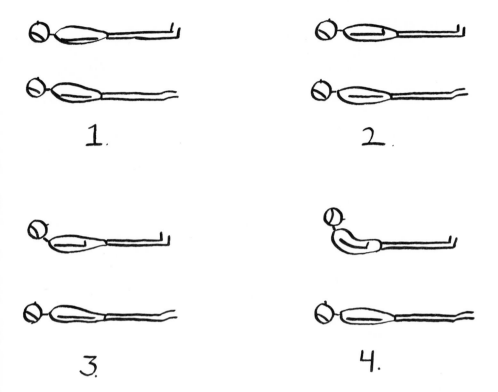

1.  2.

3.  4.

**Fig. 3-11**

## CHANGES OF LEVEL

*SMALL BOUNCES*—Standing position.
1.  Bend the knees, and keeping the heels on the floor, bounce lightly. See Fig. 3-12. Repeat for sixteen counts.

**Fig. 3-12**

*BOBS*—Straddle stand, hands on the hips.
   1.  Bend over and keeping the legs straight, reach for the floor. Bob gently in
       this position sixteen counts.
   2.  Stand, place the hands on the hips, tilt the head backward, and lean
       backward. Bob sixteen counts.
   3.  Return to an erect position, lift the right arm overhead, extending the left
       arm down next to the side. Lean to the left and bob sixteen counts.
   4.  Exchange arm positions and lean to the right and bob sixteen counts. See
       Fig. 3-13.
   Repeat the sequence with eight, four, two and one counts of bobbing each
   time.

**Fig. 3-13**

*KNEE BOBS*—Standing position, with the trunk bent enough so that the hands
   can be placed on the knees.
   1. & 2.  Keeping the legs straight, press backward on the knees two counts.
   3. & 4.  Squat down, and keeping the heels flat on the floor bounce twice.
            See Fig. 3-14.
   Repeat.

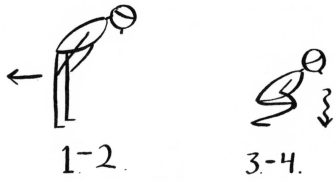

**Fig. 3-14**

*ARM SWINGS*—Straddle stand with the arms at the sides.
1. Swing the arms forward and up, reaching as high as possible.
2. Swing the arms down and back, and at the same time bend forward at the waist until the arms are reaching for the ceiling over the back of the body.
3. Straighten the body and swing the arms forward and up again.
4. Return the arms to the sides. See Fig. 3-15.

**Fig. 3-15**

*BOUNCES*—Standing position with the arms at the sides.
1.  Jump in place for four counts.
2.  Jump in the straddle stand position with the arms raised parallel to the floor at shoulder level two counts.
3.  Bring the legs together and the arms back to the sides and jump in place two counts. See Fig. 3-16.

**Fig. 3-16**

**Fig. 3-17**

*SQUARE*—Hurdle sitting position.
  1.  Bend forward and place the hands on the floor in front of the body.
  2. & 3. Stretch out on the stomach and roll onto the back.
  4.  Sit up and resume the hurdle position with the other leg in front. See Fig. 3-17.

*STANDING LEG STRETCH*—Slight straddle stand.
  1.  Place the hands on the knees.
  2.  Slide the hands down to the ankles keeping the legs straight.
  3. & 4. Stand up straight and place the hands behind the hips.
  5. & 6. Shift the hips forward by applying pressure with the hands.
  7. & 8. Place the hands at the sides and return to an erect stand. See Fig. 3-18.

**Fig. 3-18**

*SQUAT THRUSTS*—Standing position, arms at the sides.
  1.  Squat, placing the hands on the floor, shoulder width apart.
  2.  Push the feet off the floor and extend the legs backward, landing in a push-up position.
  3.  Return to the squat position.
  4.  Return to a stand. See Fig. 3-19.

**Fig. 3-19**

*BODY WAVE*—Kneeling position with the body erect and the arms hanging at the sides.
  1.        Bend forward, contracting the body until the forehead reaches the knees.
  2,3,4.    Slowly straighten the body by straightening the spine, one vertebrá at a time, from the lower back on up to the neck, the head coming erect last.
  5.        Lean backward from the knees, letting the head fall back.
  6,7,8.    Bring the body erect slowly by gradually shifting the body weight back over the knees, bringing the head erect last. See Fig. 3-20.

*PUSH UP AND ARCH*—Front lying position with the hands under the shoulders and the arms straight as in a push-up.
  1.  Bend the arms and lower the chest to the floor and at the same time raise the right leg as high as possible off the floor.
  2.  Return to the starting position.
  3.  Lower the chest again, lifting the left leg.
  4.  Return to the starting position. See Fig. 3-21.

*SIT-UPS AND ARCHES*—Back lying position, arms overhead.
  1.  Sit up, touching the fingers to the toes.
  2.  Return to the back lying position with the arms overhead.
  3.  Roll over on to the stomach.
  4.  Arch the back, lifting the head, shoulders, extended arms, and legs as high off the floor as possible.

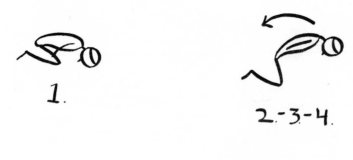

1.

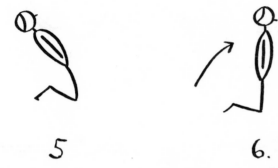

2.-3.-4.

5

6.

Fig. 3-20

1.

2.

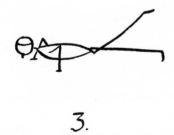

3.

4.

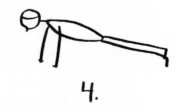

Fig. 3-21

5. Lower the body to the floor.
6. Roll to the back lying position. See Fig. 3-22.

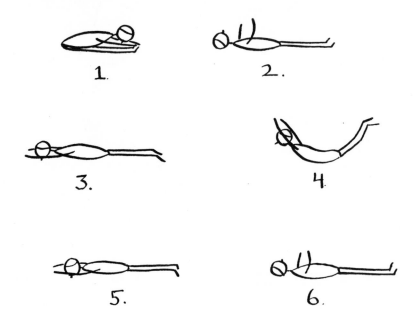

**Fig. 3-22**

*ANKLE FLEXIONS*—Straddle standing position, arms lifted sideward and held
    parallel to the floor at shoulder level.
1. Bend the knees.
2. Lift the heels up off the floor and balance on the balls of the feet.
3. Straighten the legs at the knees.
4. Lower the heels to the floor.
5. Lift the heels off the floor and balance on the balls of the feet.
6. Bend the knees.
7. Lower the heels to the floor.
8. Straighten the legs. See Fig. 3-23.

*KNEE STRETCH*—Standing position, with the trunk bent slightly forward and
    the hands on the knees.
    1. & 2. Press back on the knees.
    3. & 4. Squat down and bounce with the heels flat.
    5. & 6. Step forward with the left foot into a lunge position; lift the arms
            sideward and parallel to the floor and bounce two counts with the
            weight over the forward foot.
    7. & 8. Return to a stand and bring the arms back to the sides. See Fig. 3-24.
    Repeat to the other side.

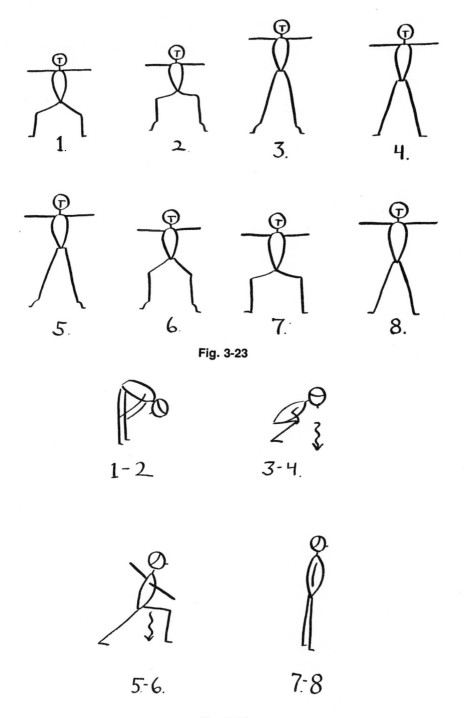

Fig. 3-23

Fig. 3-24

*SQUAT STRETCH*—Standing position, arms at the sides.
1. Squat.
2. Place the seat on the floor and lean back into a back lying position with the legs extended and the arms overhead.
3. Sit up, tuck, and return to a squat.
4. Stand. See Fig. 3-25.

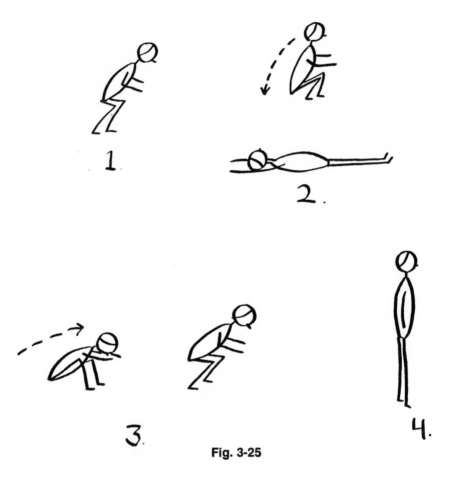

**Fig. 3-25**

*STANDING SQUARE*—Standing position.
1. & 2. Place the left foot back one step and lower the body into a hurdle sit with the right foot in front.
3.       Bend forward and place the hands on the floor in front of the body.
4. & 5. Stretch out on the stomach and roll on to the back.
6.       Sit up into a hurdle sit with the left leg in front.
7. & 8. Place the left foot on the floor and, taking the weight onto the left foot, stand. See Fig. 3-26.

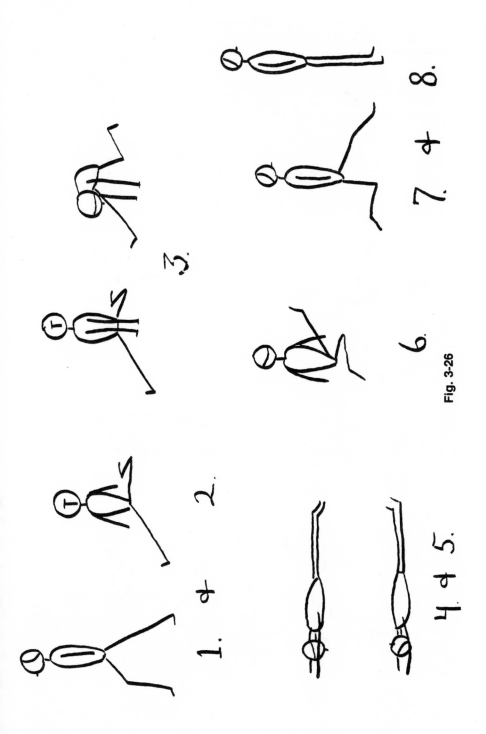

Fig. 3-26

**Fig. 3-27**

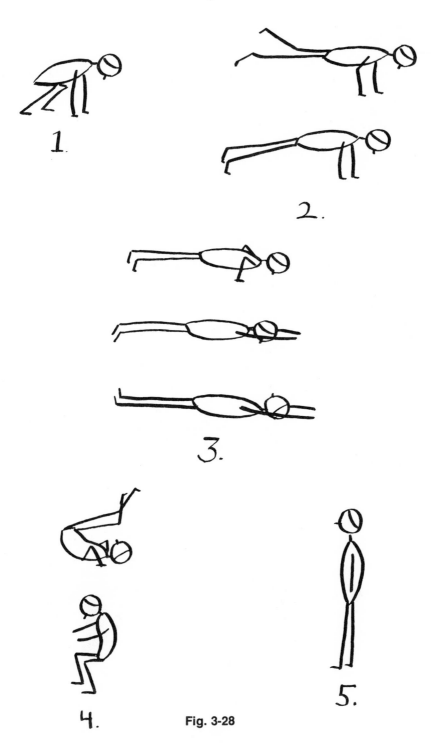

Fig. 3-28

*SQUAT, STRETCH, STRADDLE*—Standing position, with the hands on the
  hips.
  1.  Squat, placing the hands on the floor in front of the body.
  2.  Spring off the feet, extending the legs and landing in a push-up position.
  3.  Keeping the hands on the floor, spring off the feet, lifting the hips and
      landing in a straddle position.
  4.  Spring again and return to the push-up position.
  5.  Spring to a squat.
  6.  Stand in the starting position. See Fig. 3-27.

*SQUAT, SUPPORT, ROLL*—Standing position, arms at the sides.
  1.  Squat, placing the hands on the floor in front of the body.
  2.  Spring off the feet and extend the legs, landing in a push-up position,
      keeping the arms straight.
  3.  Lower the body to the floor and extend the arms overhead. Roll one
      complete revolution, ending on the stomach.
  4.  Place the hands under the shoulders and spring to a squat.
  5.  Stand. See Fig. 3-28.

## CHANGES OF DIRECTION

*SIDE STRETCH*—Straddle standing position, with the arms at the sides.
  1.  Place the left hand on the left hip and let the right hand slide down the
      right leg as the body leans to the right.
  2.  Return to a stand.
  3.  Lift the left hand overhead and let the right arm slide down the right leg as
      the body bends again to the right.
  4.  Return to a stand. See Fig. 3-29.

  Repeat to the other side.

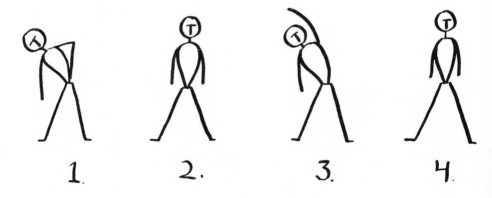

**Fig. 3-29**

*SIDE BENDS*—Straddle standing position with the arms raised to shoulder level and held parallel to the floor.
1. Lift the left arm overhead and slide the right arm down the right leg as the body leans to the right.
2. Return to a stand, keeping the arms parallel.
3. Let the arms swing down and cross in front of the body.
4. Lift the arms back up to shoulder level. See Fig. 3-30.

Repeat leaning to the other side.

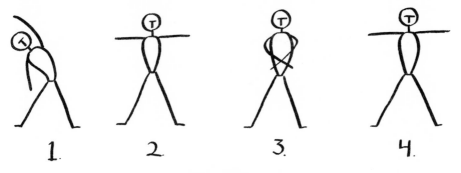

**Fig. 3-30**

*TRUNK TWIST*—Standing position, arms at the sides.
1. Swing the arms forward and up until they are at shoulder level and are parallel to the floor.
2. Swing the arms to the left side, letting the right arm cross in front of the body and twisting the trunk.
3. Swing the arms back to center and rotate the trunk back to the forward position.
4. Lower the arms to the sides. See Fig. 3-31.

Repeat to the other side.

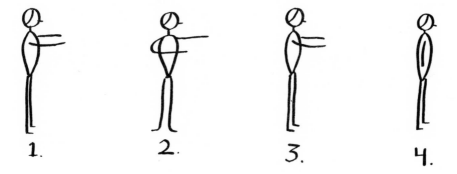

**Fig. 3-31**

*MARCH*—Standing position with the feet in parallel position.
1. Lift the arms sideward to shoulder level, parallel to the floor and lift the right leg until the upper leg is parallel to the floor.
2. Lower the raised leg and let the arms swing down and across in front of the body.
3. Lift the arms again and at the same time lift the left leg.
4. Return to the standing position. See Fig. 3-32.

**Fig. 3-32**

*HIP STRETCH*—Straddle standing position, arms at the sides.
1. Place the right hand on the right knee and the left hand on the left hip as the body bends to the right. Keep the knees straight and the heels on the floor.
2. Return to the standing position.
3. & 4. Keeping the arms straight, move them in a circle backward, overhead, and return them to the sides by passing in front of the body. See Fig. 3-33.

Repeat leaning to the other side.

**Fig. 3-33**

*CIRCLE AND BEND*—Straddle standing position with the arms at the sides.

1. & 2. Keeping the arms straight and parallel to each other move them in a complete circle to the left, moving in front of the body and overhead back to the starting position.

3. & 4. Continue the movement of the left arm until it is overhead again, and letting the right arm slide down the right leg, lean sideward to the right and bob twice.

5. & 6. Circle the arms to the right.

7. & 8. Bob to the left. See Fig. 3-34.

*FLANK TURN*—Long sitting position, hands on the knees.

1. Place the hands on the floor to the right side of the body and lean onto the right hip.

2. & 3. Taking the weight on the hands, lift the hips, and keeping the legs straight circle them around behind and place them on the floor next to the hands and rest the weight on the left hip.

4. Lower the body into the long sit position. See Fig. 3-35.

Repeat to the other side.

## MOVING THROUGH SPACE

*FOUR JUMPS*—Standing position, arms at the sides.

1. Jump four times in place.

2. Run four steps forward. See Fig. 3-36.

Repeat.

*HOPS*—Standing position, arms at the sides.

1. Hop four times on the right foot.

2. Run forward four steps.

3. Hop four times on the left foot.

4. Run forward four steps.

Be sure to hop in one place each time. See Fig. 3-37.

*STRADDLE JUMPS AND RUNS*—Standing position, arms at the sides.

1. Jump to a side stride position.

2. Jump and land with the feet together.

3. & 4. Repeat 1 and 2.

5. Run forward four steps. See Fig. 3-38.

*STEP SKIPS*—Standing position, arms at the sides.

1. Step onto the right foot.

2. Skip on the left foot.

3. & 4. Hop twice on the right foot in place.

5. Step onto the left foot.

6. Skip on the right foot.

7. & 8. Hop twice on the left foot in place. See Fig. 3-39.

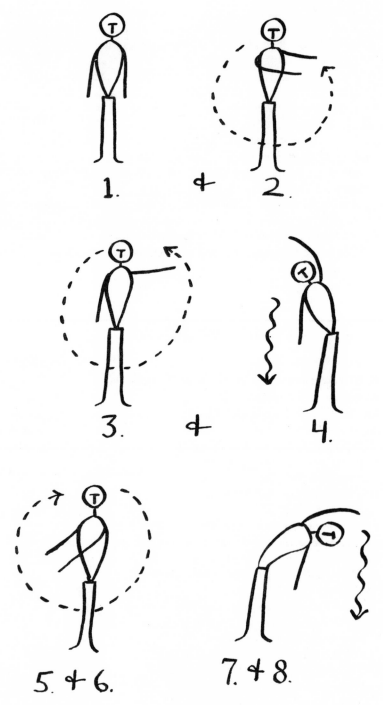

**Fig. 3-34**

1.

2.

+

3.

4.

**Fig. 3-35**

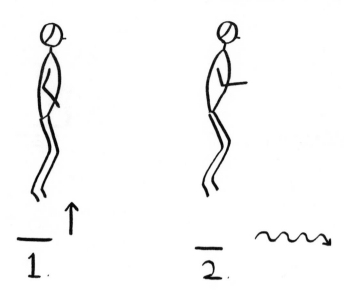

**Fig. 3-36**

**Fig. 3-37**

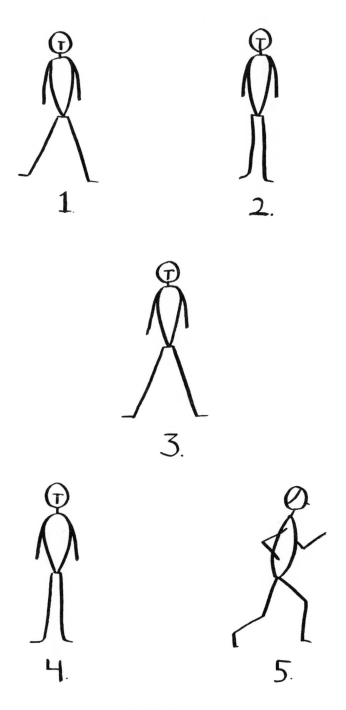

Fig. 3-38

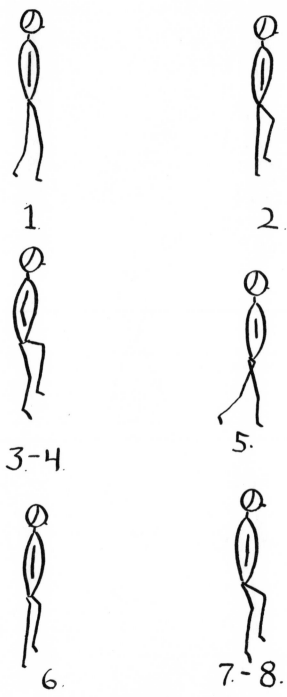

1.

2.

3-4.

5.

6.

7.-8.

**Fig. 3-39**

*FRONT, SIDE, FRONT, TOGETHER*—Standing position, feet together, arms at the sides.

1. Hop on the left foot, landing with the right foot pointed on the floor in front of the body and the arms raised forward to shoulder height.
2. Hop on the left foot again, landing with the right foot pointed on the floor to the right side of the body and the arms opened to shoulder height and pointed sideward.
3. Hop on the left foot again, pointing the right foot forward and returning the arms to the front shoulder height position.
4. Hop on the left foot and land in the starting position. See Fig. 3-40.

Repeat, hopping on the right foot and extending the left in the same pattern.

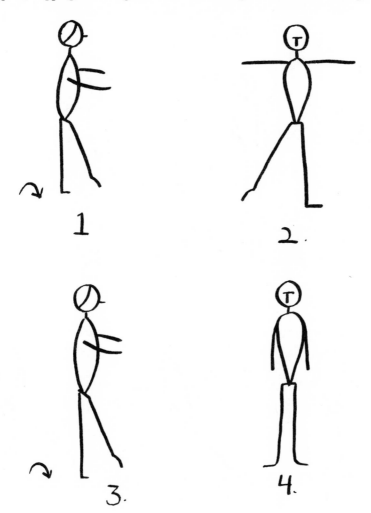

**Fig. 3-40**

Fig. 3-41

*STRADDLE JUMPS*—Standing position with the arms at the sides.
1. Jump to a side straddle position, lifting the arms sideward to shoulder level.
2. Jump and land in the starting position.
3. Jump to the stride position with the right foot forward and the left foot back, lifting the left arm forward to shoulder level and the right arm back.
4. Jump and land in the starting position.
5. Jump to a straddle position, lifting the arms sideward to shoulder level.
6. Jump and land in the starting position.
7. Jump to a stride position with the left foot forward and the right foot back, lifting the right arm forward to shoulder level and the left arm back.
8. Jump to the starting position. See Fig. 3-41.

## FOR FURTHER REFERENCE

*Adult Physical Fitness*. Washington D.C., President's Council on Physical Fitness, n.d.

Cooper, K. H., *The New Aerobics*. Philadelphia, Lippencott, 1970.

Edmonds, I. G., *Isometric and Isotonic Exercises for Men and Women*. Cerby, Connecticut, Monarch, 1964.

*Fitness for Living*. Emmaus, Pennsylvania, Rodale Press, n.d.

Kuntzleman, C. T., *Physical Fitness Encyclopedia*. Emmaus, Pennsylvania, Rodale Press, 1970.

Rosandich, T., Ward, & Lawson, *The American Training Patterns*. Upson, Wisconsin, Olympia Sport, n.d.

*Royal Canadian Air Force Exercise Plans for Physical Fitness*. Ottawa, Royal Canadian Air Force, 1962.

Vitale, F., *Individualized Fitness Programs*. Englewood Cliffs, New Jersey, Prentice-Hall, Inc., 1973.

Wallis, E. L., and G. A. Logan, *Figure Improvement and Body Conditioning Through Exercise*. Englewood Cliffs, New Jersey, Prentice-Hall, Inc., 1964.

# 4

# MOVING OVER, UNDER, AROUND, AND THROUGH: OBSTACLE COURSES

Though many areas of physical functioning can be developed solely through exercise, the real test of whether or not this development has taken place is in having these various areas function together. Strength is useless unless the body also has the balance to maintain the necessary physical position. Speed is wasted if the joint flexibility to permit full range of motion is not present. Essentially, the person must be able to first, combine his capabilities in terms of strength, flexibility, balance, endurance, and speed; and second, to use these combined capabilities in a variety of movement situations. Obstacle courses require a person to do this.

Because they are constructed entirely by the teacher to meet the needs of the students involved, obstacle courses can be made as easy or as difficult as desired. They can contain anywhere from one to a dozen obstacles, each only as challenging as the teacher feels is necessary. Because they are made up of separate, individual items they can be changed at will as the ability of the students increases. Obstacles can be made out of virtually any object in the room. It may be a familiar piece of gymnastic equipment used in an unfamiliar way, classroom furniture, or homemade odds and ends.

This chapter contains lists of the various items which can be used for obstacles. In addition, the specific physical activity which may be used to overcome each obstacle is included. Where there is an alternate to a suggested piece listed, it is an indication that there are several possibilities open to the teacher based on what materials are available to him.

Following the lists of obstacles are ten sample courses. They are meant to stimulate the creative thinking of the reader, for any obstacle course can be as different and challenging as one wishes to make it. As will be illustrated, expensive equipment is not needed. The teacher should feel free to adjust the sample courses to fit his situation, changing spacing or adjusting distance as needed. For additional reference on the stunts listed, the reader should refer to Chapter 5.

Some additional hints:

1. Once constructed, each course should be checked for safety hazards.
2. Provide spotters at difficult or confusing areas.
3. Use tape arrows or signs to show directions.
4. Once the course is familiar, have students race against their own time.
5. Increase the length and difficulty of the course as the physical capability of the students increases.

## IMPROVISING WITH SIMPLE EQUIPMENT

### BENCH:

1. Walk with one foot on the bench and one foot on the floor.
2. Crawl under.
3. Use as a wide balance beam.
4. Step on and jump off.
5. Place the hands on bench and jump over without letting the feet or legs touch.
6. Place a mat over the bench and dive and roll over it.

### BOXES:

1. Step into a box and then out of it with both feet.
2. Walk, stepping with one foot into each box.
3. Use as obstacles to run around.
4. Cut the bottoms out and crawl through.
5. Cut the bottom out, step into the box and lift it off over the head.

## CHAIRS:

1. Crawl under.
2. Crawl under, lying on one's back.
3. Crawl under, feet first.
4. Step onto the seat and back off to the floor.
5. Suspend wands or rope between two chairs and step or jump over.
6. Suspend wands or rope between two chairs and step or jump over backward.
7. Suspend two ropes at different heights and crawl between them.
8. Use as an object to run around.
9. Use a folding chair and crawl between the seat and the back.

## CONES:

1. Use as an obstacle to run around.
2. Suspend a pole or rope between two cones and use in the same way that you did for chairs.
3. Use as support for mats to make a tunnel.

## LADDER:

1. Walk to the other end with one foot on each side piece of the ladder.
2. Walk to the other end, placing one foot on each rung.
3. Walk or run to the other end, placing one foot into each space between the rungs.
4. Stand on one end of the ladder, place one foot on each side piece, place hands on ladder and walk on hands and feet to other end.
5. Starting at one end of the ladder, jump, landing in each space between the rungs.
6. Walk backward from one end to the other, placing one foot into each space between the rungs.
7. Walk backward from one end to the other with one foot on each side piece.
8. Jump backward from one end to the other landing in each space between the rungs.
9. Jump sideward from one end to the other landing in each space between the rungs.
10. Walk sideward stepping into each rung space first with the lead foot and then the other foot. Each foot touches the ground in each space.
11. Walk sideward, stepping into one rung space with the lead foot and stepping across to the next rung space with the trail foot.
12. With the ladder lying on its side (it may be necessary to have someone

hold the ends) crawl through one rung space, turn and crawl back through the next one to the other end.

## ROPE:

1. Anchor one end of a long rope (over 8') securely, about one and one-half feet off the ground. Stretch out the rope perpendicular to the anchoring point. Lie on the floor and pull from the loose end to the anchoring point.
2. Use for locomotor rope skipping over marked distance. Refer to Chapter 7 for specific stunts.
3. Suspend between two stationary objects and crawl under or jump over.

## TAPE:

1. Use for start and finish markers.
2. Line a tunnel with two strips approximately one foot apart and five feet long. Jump from side to side, traveling forward also, for the length of the tunnel. Landing should be outside the tape lines.
3. Use to mark an area in which a stunt is to be performed.
4. Form geometric shapes on the floor and use as landing areas for jumping, hopping or running. Performer should land with feet (or foot) inside the area bounded by the tape.
5. Use for arrows to show direction.

## TIRES:

1. Arrange tires in two parallel lines close to each other. Run from one end of the line to the other placing one foot in each tire.
2. Have extra students hold tires in an upright position. Performer then crawls through the holes.
3. Place tires in a single line and hop from one end to the other.
4. Arrange in a pattern requiring a variety of hopping and jumping.
5. Roll the tire and run along side of it.
6. Crawl half way through a tire and roll sidewards while lying in it.
7. Step into the tire hole. Pull the tire up over the head.

## WANDS OR SHORT POLES:

1. Pick up wand with both hands and holding it in front of you, step through it.
2. Hold wand in front of you and jump through it.
3. Suspend wand between two chairs and resting on the seats. Go over without touching the pole.
4. Suspend wand between rungs under two chairs. Crawl under.

## USING APPARATUS

### *BALANCE BEAM:*

(A 2″ x 4″ or 4″ x 4″ plank eight feet long may be substituted.)

1. Go from one end to the other by any means possible. Do not touch the floor.
2. Go from one end to the other by any means possible moving backward. Do not touch the floor.
3. Approach from the side and go over the beam in any manner.
4. Approach from the side and go over without using the hands.
5. Approach from the side and go over without letting the legs or feet touch the beam.
6. Approach from the side and do a forward roll over the beam.
7. Straddle sit on one end, and using hands and legs work to the other end.
8. String a rope from one end of the beam supports to the other end and halfway between the beam and the floor. Approach from the side and go between the rope and the beam without touching either the rope or the beam.
9. Hang on the underside of the beam at one end. Work down to the other end, staying under the beam.

### *HORIZONTAL LADDER:*

1. Hang by both hands at one end and work to the other end going hand-over-hand on the rungs.
2. Hang by both hands at one end. With the hands on the sides of the ladder work down to the other end.
3. Start by hanging at one end. Crawl up between the first two rungs of the ladder and crawl on top of the ladder to the other end. Then lower the body back down to the ground through the space between the last two rungs.
4. Start by hanging at one end. Crawl up through the first two rungs. Go over a rung and down between the next two. Keep going up and down making an over and under pattern with the rungs. End by going down between the last two.
5. Hang at one end, with both hands on the same side of the ladder. Move sideward down to the other end.
6. Hang by hands and knees at one end. Work down to the other end using hands and legs while hanging under the ladder.

## LONG HORSE OR VAULT BOX:

(A desk or table may be substituted.)
1. Climb on to a standing position and jump off.
2. Go over any way possible.
3. Climb on to a standing position, turn around and jump off backward.
4. Climb on to a standing position, turn around and jump off backward. While in the air turn and land facing forward.
5. Climb onto one end. From a squat position do a forward somersault toward the other end.
6. Lay across the horse on your stomach. Place the hands on the floor and roll off through a forward somersault.

## MATS:

(An old mattress may be substituted.)
1. Roll the mat and use it as an obstacle to jump over.
2. Roll a mat loosely and crawl through the tunnel it makes.
3. Suspend a mat between two chairs and crawl under it.
4. Place a mat over the horizontal bar or parallel bars (it may be necessary to tie it in place), and crawl over it.
5. Use as a floor covering for stunt performance.

## PARALLEL BARS:

1. Push up to a front support on one end and walk to the other end.
2. Push to a front support on one end. Swing the legs forward and place one leg over each bar. Keeping the legs straight and the toes pointed place the hands on the bars ahead of the legs. Lift the hips and swing the legs over the bars behind you. As the legs swing down continue the momentum and repeat the exercise, traveling to the other end of the bars.
3. Set the bars as high as possible. At one end hang by the hands and feet under one bar and work along the bar to the other end.
4. Set the bars as high as possible. At one end hang with hands on one bar and legs over the other. Work along both bars to the other end.
5. Approach the bars from the side. Climb over both bars to the other side.
6. Approach the bars from the side. Climb over the first bar, under the second, and then back over the first without touching the floor.
7. Set one bar high and one low. Starting at the end, support with one arm and hang with the other and progress to the other end.

8. Set one bar low and one high. Approach from the low side and crawl over both bars.
9. Place a mat over the bars. Crawl through the tunnel formed from one to the other.

## RINGS:

1. Grasp both rings. Tuck the legs and turn over forwards in a somersault. Tuck agan and return to starting position.
2. Grasp both rings and do a backward somersault and return to the starting position.
3. Grasp both rings and let the rest of the body hang. Place the feet directly under the rings and straighten the legs. Then swivel the body around in a full circle with the feet and hands forming the pivot for the long axis of the body.
4. Grasp both rings. Tuck the legs and place the feet through the rings up to the knees. Let go with the hands and hang by the knees. Regrasp the rings and return to a stand.
5. Grasp the rings with both hands and pull up to a chin-up position.

## ROPE:

(A piece of hemp hung from a football crossbar may be substituted.)
1. Place two mats on the floor, one under the end of the rope and the other approximately eight feet away. Swing from one mat to the other.
2. Perform the above but swing over a rope or pole suspended horizontally approximately three feet off the ground.
3. Climb the rope.
4. Lie on your back under the end of the rope. Using only the arms, pull to a standing position.
5. Grasp the rope in front of you with both hands. Keeping the rope between the legs lift the legs off the ground and over the body until they are parallel to the floor. Hang in this pike position.
6. Grasp the rope in front of you with both hands. Lift the legs and place the feet on the rope above the hands. Slide the feet up the rope until the body is completely inverted.

## STALL BARS OR VERTICAL LADDER:

1. Walk up and down the bars.
2. Hang from one of the high bars and pull up to a chin-up position.
3. Walk up the bars using the arms only.

## SAMPLE COURSES

### *SIMPLE EQUIPMENT COURSE–1*

1. Run through the row of tires, stepping once into each tire.
2. Crawl under the wand.
3. Walk the length of the plank.
4. Run around once in a circle.
5. Jump on two feet from square to square.
6. Seal walk between the tape lines.
7. Lie on back, grasp rope and pull head first till it is possible to touch the anchoring point.
8. Run over the poles and continue running to the finish line. See Fig. 4-1.

### *SIMPLE EQUIPMENT COURSE–2*

1. Walk across the plank.
2. Hold the pole in two hands in front of the body. Step (or jump) across and back without letting go of the pole.
3. Walk on hands and feet, using the rungs of the ladder. Go from one end to the other.
4. Crawl under to the side.
5. Run miniature shuttle run.
6. Walk, stepping with one foot into each box.
7. Crawl under the first pole, over the second, under the third and over the fourth.
8. Long jump from first tape line to the second.
9. Walk with one foot on the bench and one foot on the floor.
10. Jump on two feet in a zig-zag pattern. Land first on one side of the tape lines and then the other. See Fig. 4-2.

### *SIMPLE EQUIPMENT COURSE–3*

1. Crawl under the tunnel of chairs.
2. Walk backward, stepping into each rung space.
3. Run in a zig-zag pattern around the outside of each chair.
4. Walk on hands and feet, right hand and foot on the right tape line, left hand and foot on left tape line.
5. Log roll from the first tape line to the second.
6. Crawl through the hole in each tire.
7. Pick up the rope and skip rope to the tape line.
8. Pick up each wand, hold it with both hands and jump through it. See Fig. 4-3.

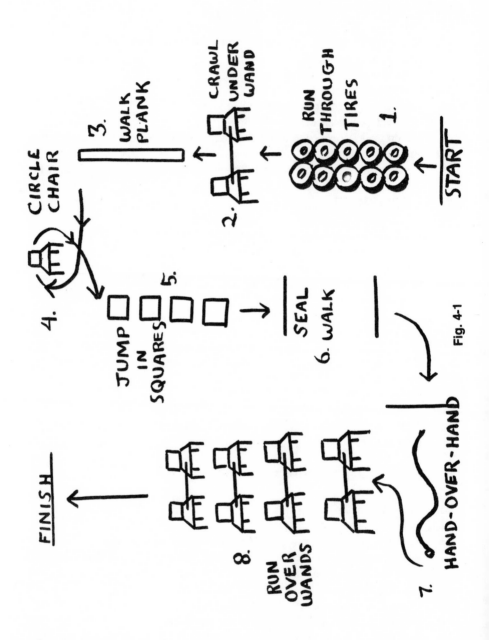

Fig. 4-1

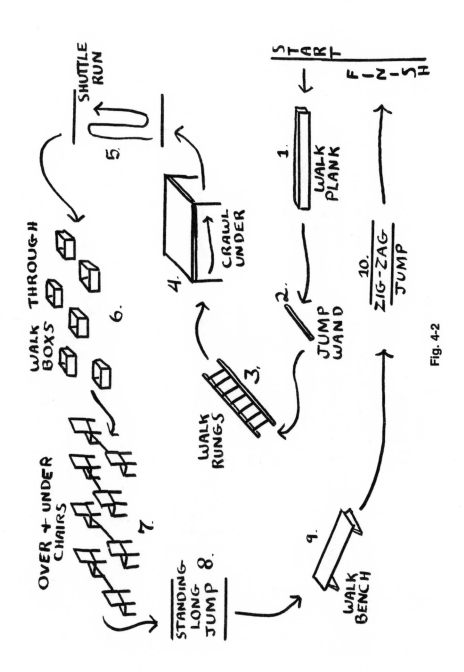

Fig. 4-2

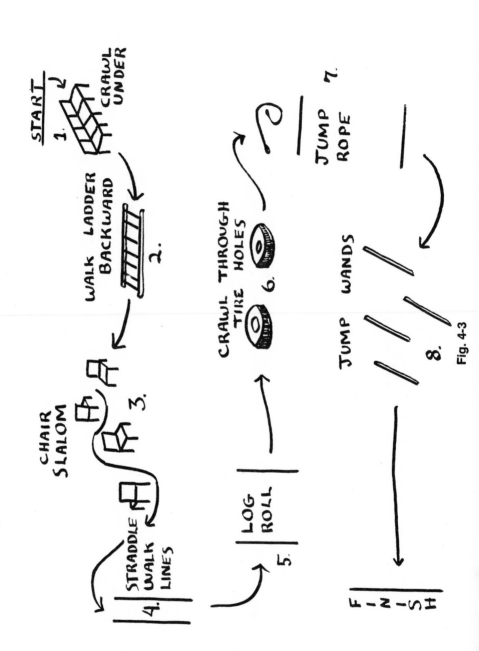

Fig. 4-3

## SPORTS COURSE

1. Forward roll, backward roll, forward roll.
2. Run, placing one foot into each tire hole.
3. Dribble basketball style around the cones.
4. Long jump from one tape line to the other.
5. Push up and walk on arms from one end to the other.
6. Dribble soccer style around the cones.
7. Run the bases.
8. Run the low hurdles. See Fig. 4-4.

## PARTNER COURSE

1. Three partner forward rolls.
2. Wheelbarrow to tape line and back.
3. One person forms a bridge and the other person crawls under. Reverse places and repeat. Each person should be a bridge twice.
4. Leap frog.
5. Camel walk length of mat.
6. One person steps into the square and then catches a ball thrown by her partner. Then the other person steps into the parallel square and catches the ball her partner returns to her. Repeat to the end of the line of squares and back.
7. Tandem the length of mat.
8. Link arms and run to finish line. See Fig. 4-5.

## OUTDOOR COURSE

1. Slalom run around cones.
2. Run low hurdles.
3. Run up and down the bleachers.
4. Jump and touch object suspended from the football crossbar.
5. Run through the tires, stepping once into each tire.
6. Jump in a zig-zag pattern the length of the long jump runway. Land on either side of the runway, not on it.
7. Run through the pit.
8. Step on either side of the runway or lines in another zig-zag pattern.
9. Slalom backward around the cones. See Fig. 4-6.

## APPARATUS COURSE–1

1. Forward somersault and return to starting position.
2. Crawl through the tunnel made by covering the parallel bars with a mat.
3. Walk with body touching the stall bars.

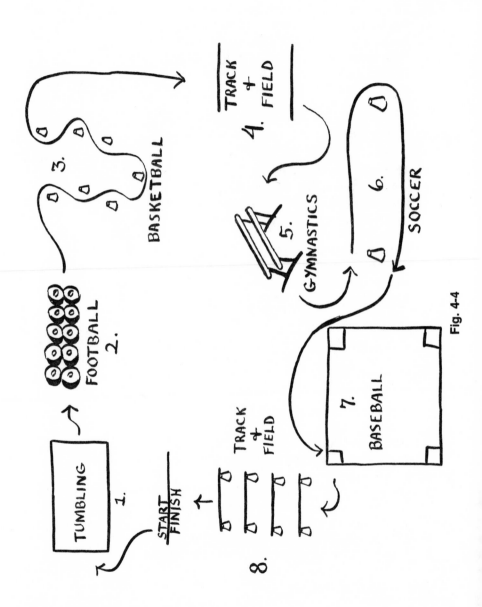

Fig. 4-4

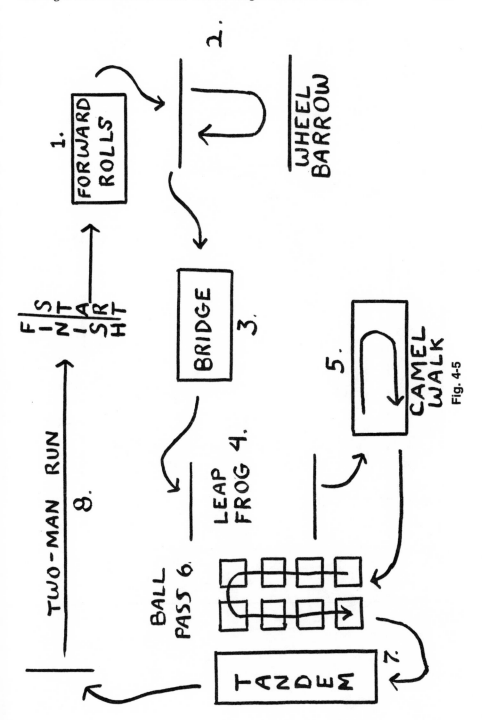

Fig. 4-5

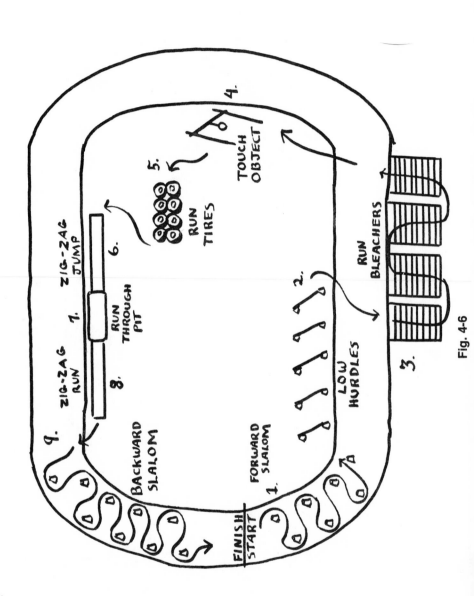

Fig. 4-6

4. Walk across the beam.
5. Go over the horse or vault box, passing both legs to one side.
6. Push up and walk hand over hand to the other end.
7. Crawl over the horizontal bar covered by a mat.
8. Go over the buck, passing feet between the hands.
9. Hang and move hand over hand along the rungs.
10. Swing from the take off mat to the landing mat. See Fig. 4-7.

## APPARATUS COURSE-2

1. Crab walk from starting line to next tape line.
2. Chin-up on the rings.
3. Hop on one foot through the line of tires.
4. Place the stomach on the vault box or horse. Place the hands on the mat on other side. Front somersault over.
5. Crawl on hands and knees on the beam.
6. Crawl over the bars.
7. Miniature shuttle run between tape lines.
8. Crawl through the tunnel made by a rolled up mat.
9. Side slide from tape to finish line. See Fig. 4-8.

## APPARATUS COURSE-3

1. Hang and walk hand over hand from one end to the other.
2. Jump, landing on both feet, into each tape square.
3. Crawl under the tunnel made by resting the corners of a mat on chairs.
4. Pick up rope and jump through it.
5. Climb on vaulting box, stand up and jump off.
6. Back shoulder roll the length of mats.
7. Push up at one end. Swing legs up and over bars into a straddle position, one on each bar. Place hands ahead of legs. Swing legs over the bars and behind the performer (by lifting the hips). Repeat to end of bars.
8. Run in a weaving pattern around the cones.
9. Crawl between the ropes. See Fig. 4-9.

## APPARATUS COURSE-4

1. Push up and walk backward on hands to other end.
2. Walk backward over wands suspended between chairs.
3. Walk on hands and feet on ladder rungs to other end.
4. Crawl over the box without letting legs touch.
5. Crawl under chairs, lying on back.
6. Stand with feet directly under rings. Swivel body in one complete circle. (Rings should be at approximately shoulder height.)

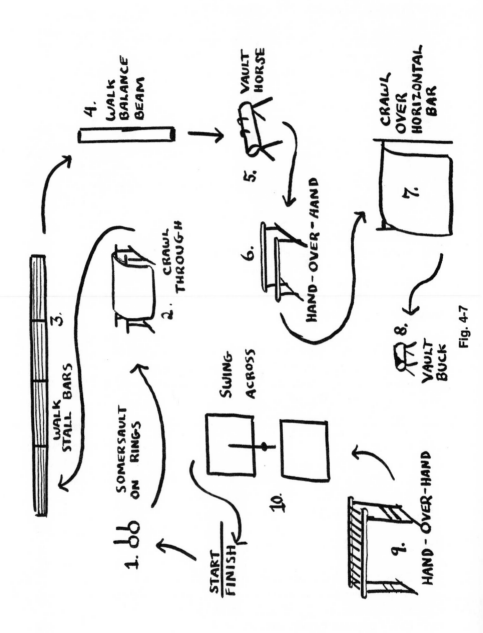

Fig. 4-7

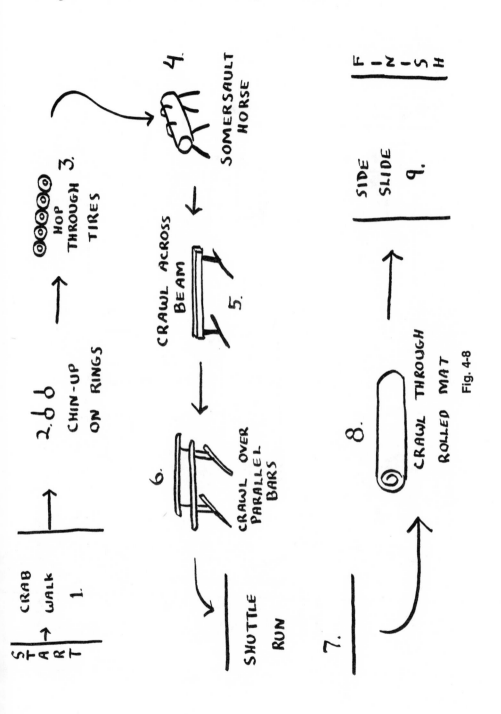

Fig. 4-8

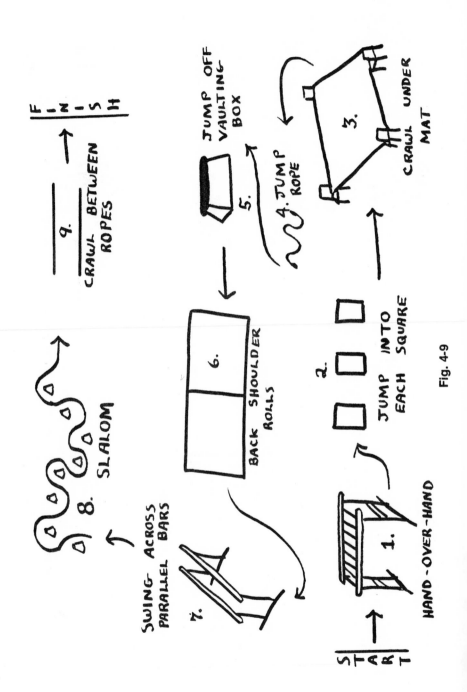

Fig. 4-9

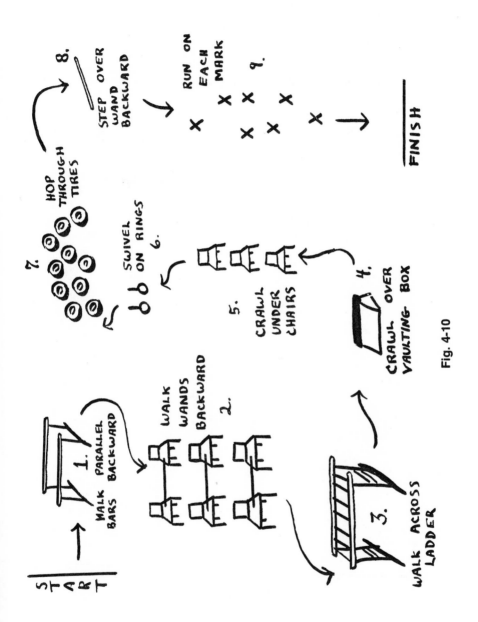

Fig. 4-10

7. Alternately hop on one foot and jump on two through the tires.
8. Pick up and step backward through the wand.
9. Run, placing one foot on each tape X. See Fig. 4-10.

## FOR FURTHER REFERENCE

Diem, Liselott, *Who Can* . . . Frankfort, Germany, Limpert, 1957.

Morison, Ruth, *A Movement Approach to Educational Gymnastics*. London, Dent, 1969.

Mosston, Muska, *Developmental Movement*. Columbus, Merrill, 1965.

# 5

# WORKING ON MATS
# TO PROMOTE COORDINATION

Once the factors of balance, strength, flexibility, and endurance start to improve the student needs to begin to apply his capabilities in some of the more traditional physical education activities. Coordination as an intrinsic accomplishment has little value. It is only when this accomplishment has been applied successfully that its true benefit can be gained. Simple tumbling activities provide an excellent means of not only applying what coordination has been developed in a more challenging way but also of demanding further development of the physical factors involved.

Most of the activities in this chapter are slightly more difficult than the exercises already described. They require a greater degree of not only strength and flexibility but particularly they require more balance. It is because of this increase in difficulty that it is suggested that the student initially attempt the performance of these activities on a mat rather than on the bare floor. Students with coordination problems are more likely to experience difficulties during the initial learning phase of the stunts, and using a mat will not only prevent injuries but also provide security for the unsure student.

The stunts are grouped into four categories: those whose main physical requirement is balance; simple stunt activities; rolls; and activities designed for two or more people working together. Each are listed in progressive order within each group. The student should be encouraged to master as many stunts in each category as possible. Even though initial attempts may be frustrating most of the activities are easy enough to be learned with a little practice.

## BALANCING ACTIVITIES

*ANGEL BALANCE*—Kneeling position on both hands and both knees. Extend one leg back and behind the body and extend the opposite arm forward and ahead. Keep the head up and the extended arm and leg straight. Support of the body is maintained with the other arm and leg. See Fig. 5-1.

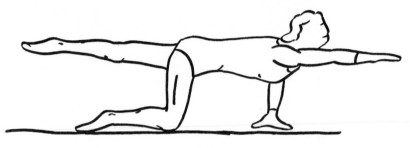

**Fig. 5-1**

*KNEE SCALE*—Kneel on both knees, placing the hands on the floor, shoulder width apart. Lift the right leg and extend it behind the body as high as possible. Lift the head and arch the back as the leg is lifted. Hold the balance with the knees and the other arm. See Fig. 5-2.

**Fig. 5-2**

*SUPINE ARCH*—Long sitting position. Place the hands behind the hips on the floor. Taking the weight on the hands and the feet, arch the back and lift the hips off the floor until the body is straight in alignment from feet to head. Continue the arch as high as possible. See Fig. 5-3.

**Fig. 5-3**

*SCALE*—Standing position. Lift the right leg to the rear as high as possible. At the same time bend the body forward and extend the arms sideward at shoulder level. Continue bending forward and lifting the leg until the body is parallel to the floor. See Fig. 5-4.

**Fig. 5-4**

*SHOULDER STAND*—Back lying position. Tuck the knees to the chest, and lifting the hips extend the legs toward the ceiling. Support of the body is on the shoulders. Raise the legs until the body is in complete extension. See Fig. 5-5.

**Fig. 5-5**

*STORK STAND*—Standing position. Place the bottom of one foot against the inside of the other knee. Extend the arms at shoulder level to aid in balance. Hold this position ten seconds. Try it with the eyes closed. See Fig. 5-6.

**Fig. 5-6**

*BRIDGE*—Back lying position with the knees bent, feet flat on the floor close to the hips. The hands are placed on the floor above the shoulders with the fingers pointing toward the body. Push up the body with the hands and legs, lifting the hips high off the floor, arching the back, and dropping the head back. Straighten the arms and legs as much as possible. See Fig. 5-7.

**Fig. 5-7**

*INDIAN STAND*—Standing position with the legs crossed at the ankles and the arms folded across the chest. Keeping the arms and legs in this position, sit down on the floor and stand up again without losing the balance. See Fig. 5-8.

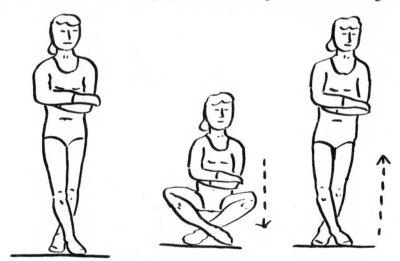

**Fig. 5-8**

*KNEE DIP*—Standing position. Bend the right leg, lifting the foot up behind the seat. Grasp the raised right foot with the right hand. Bend the standing leg and lower the body until the right knee touches the ground. Stand again without losing balance. See Fig. 5-9.

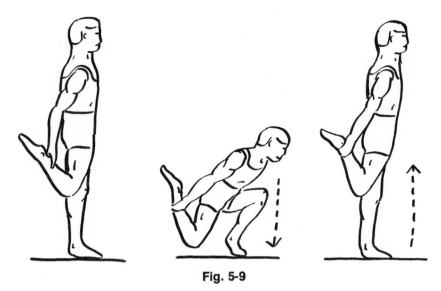

**Fig. 5-9**

*SHOOT THRU*—Lying on the stomach with the palms of the hands on the floor under the shoulders, lift the body into a front support. Push off the mat with the feet, lift the hips and tuck the legs. Then bring the legs thru the arms and extend them in front of the body. Push off again and bring the legs back thru to the starting position. See Fig. 5-10.

STARTING    POSITION

1.                                    2.

**Fig. 5-10**

*V-SEAT*—Long sitting position. Extend the arms sideward from the shoulders, parallel to the floor. Keeping the legs straight, lift them up off the floor until the body forms a "V." Lean back slightly but keep the trunk straight from hips to the shoulders. See Fig. 5-11.

**Fig. 5-11**

*TIP-UP*—Squat. Place the hands on the mat, shoulder width apart. Bend the elbows and place the knees on top of them, right to right and left to left. Keeping the head up, take the weight on the hands and lean forward until the feet are off the floor. See Fig. 5-12.

**Fig. 5-12**

*CORKSCREW*—Standing position. Place a pencil next to the outside edge of the left foot. Bend forward from the waist. Reach the right arm in front of the left leg and wrap it around the leg from the outside to inside. When the arm crosses the front of the leg for the second time pick up the pencil. See Fig. 5-13.

*PUPPY DOG STAND*—Squatting position. Place the hands on the floor, shoulder width apart, and the forehead (at the hairline) on the mat just past the hands, making the third point of a triangle. Place one knee on each elbow, lifting the feet off the floor. Balance on the hands and head. See Fig. 5-14.

Fig. 5-13

Fig. 5-14

STARTING    POSITION

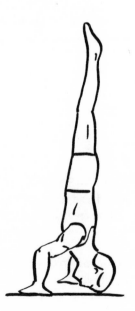

Fig. 5-15

*HEAD STAND*—Squat. Place the hands on the mat shoulder width apart. Place the head further away from the body than the hands, forming the third point of an imaginary triangle. Taking the weight on the hands and the forehead at the hairline, tuck the legs and raise them upward until the entire body is in extension. See Fig. 5-15.

*FOREARM STAND*—Squat. Place the forearms and hands on the mat in a V position pointing away from the body. Place the head on the floor between the hands, resting at approximately the hairline. Tuck the legs and lift them directly up overhead until the entire body is extended. See Fig. 5-16.

STARTING POSITION

**Fig. 5-16**

## EASY STUNTS

*SEAL WALK*—Front lying position. Place the hands under the shoulders and push up until the arms are straight. Walk on the hands, letting the rest of the body drag. See Fig. 5-17.

**Fig. 5-17**

*BEAR WALK*—Stand with the feet shoulder width apart. Bend at the waist and place the hands on the floor. Try not to bend the knees. Walk on all fours, keeping the knees as straight as possible. See Fig. 5-18.

**Fig. 5-18**

*CRAB WALK*—Sit on the floor. Bend the knees and place the feet flat on the floor close to the seat. Place the hands on the floor behind the hips. Lift the hips until the body is flat from the hips to the shoulders. Walk on all fours, keeping the trunk level in this position. See Fig. 5-19.

**Fig. 5-19**

*WALK AROUND*—Side lying position with the upper body supported by the arm closest to the floor being placed perpendicular to the floor. Keeping the body straight from feet to head, walk in a circle around the supporting hand. See Fig. 5-20.

*REVERSE WALK*—Lie on the side and support the upper part of the body on the arm placed perpendicular to the floor. Keeping the other arm resting along the other side of the body, walk backwards in a circle around the supporting hand. Try to keep the body in alignment between the feet and head. See Fig. 5-21.

*HEAD PIVOT*—Place the top of the head on the mat. Using the hands and feet for support and locomotion walk around in a circle using the head as a pivot point. See Fig. 5-22.

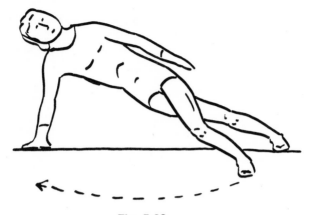

**Fig. 5-20**

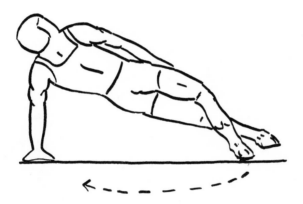

**Fig. 5-21**

**Fig. 5-22**

*TUCK JUMP*—Standing position. Jump and while in the air bring the knees to
the chest and grasp them slightly with the arms. Land in the starting position.
*KNEE WALK*—Kneel on both knees. Grasp the feet with the hands, lifting the
lower legs off the floor. Walk with the trunk upright, balanced on the knees.
See Fig. 5-23.

**Fig. 5-23**

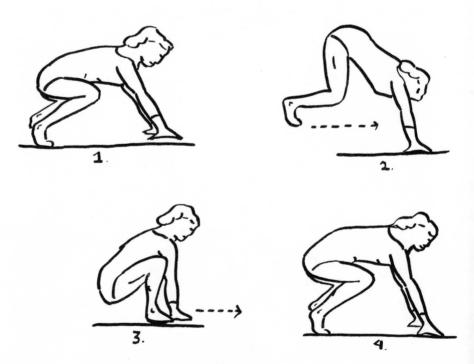

**Fig. 5-24**

*INCH WORM*—Squat and place the hands on the floor. Keeping the feet in place, walk the hands out ahead of the body until a position of full extension, such as in a push-up, is reached. Then, keeping the hands in place, lift the hips and walk the feet up to a position close to the hands. Repeat, moving first the hands and then the feet.

*FROG HOP*—Squat, placing the hands on the floor as far forward as possible. Push off with the legs and lift the hips landing with the feet close to the hands. Lift the hands and place them as far away as possible and "hop" the feet up again. Repeat. See Fig. 5-24.

*ONE LEG SQUAT*—Lift one leg upward in front of the body. Keeping this leg straight and the foot off the floor, squat on the other leg and return to a stand without losing balance. To increase the difficulty, perform the stunt with the hands on the hips. See Fig. 5-25.

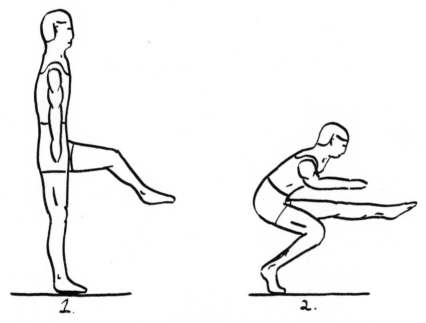

**Fig. 5-25**

*MULE KICK*—Squat, placing the hands on the floor shoulder width apart. Kick first the right leg and then quickly after, the left leg up into the air as high as possible, taking the weight on to the hands. Land in the squat.

*KNEE FALL*—Kneel on both knees, keeping the trunk upright. Maintaining body alignment from the knees to the head fall forward to the floor. Use the arms, which extend to the floor at the start of the fall and which flex at the elbow as the fall is completed, to break the fall. See Fig. 5-26.

*COURAGE JUMP*—Kneel on both knees. Using the arms for added lift and

Fig. 5-26

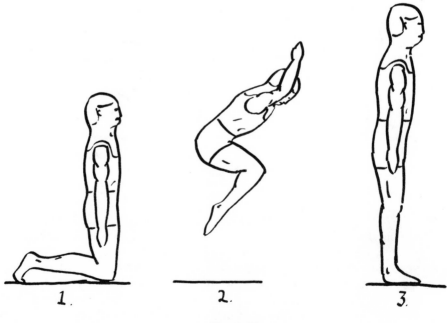

Fig. 5-27

momentum, jump to a stand. The legs and feet should leave the ground simultaneously. See Fig. 5-27.

*Variation:*

1. Perform kneeling on another object, such as a sturdy table or vault box.
2. Perform with the hands on the hips.

*TOE TOUCH*—Standing position. Jump into the air and while in the air lift the legs and attempt to touch the toes with the corresponding hands. Both the legs and arms should be kept straight, although they may be spread to the side. To enable the fingers to reach the feet the trunk flexes at the waist. Land in the starting position. See Fig. 5-28.

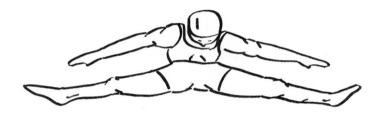

**Fig. 5-28**

*PINWHEEL*—Squat. Place the hands on the floor and extend one leg sideward. Keeping the extended leg straight, pass it under the hands, which leave the mat momentarily, and under the supporting leg, which also lifts, and circle it back to the starting position. Repeat with the other leg. See Fig. 5-29.

*FLANK TURN*—Front support position. Lift the hips slightly and circle the legs sideward. Lift one of the supporting hands momentarily to let the legs pass through and then lower the hands as the legs come to rest fully extended in front of the body with the seat over the hands. Continue the circle until the body is in the original position. Repeat in the opposite direction. See Fig. 5-30.

*HEEL CLICK*—Stand in straddle position. Jump into the air and tap the heels together once. Land with the feet in the starting position.

*Variation:*

1. Try to tap the heels together more than once.
2. While in the air, bend the knees and tap the heels together slightly to the side of the vertical body plane.

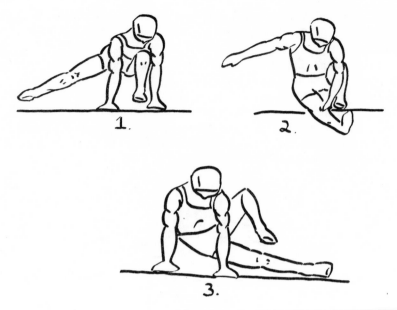

Fig. 5-29

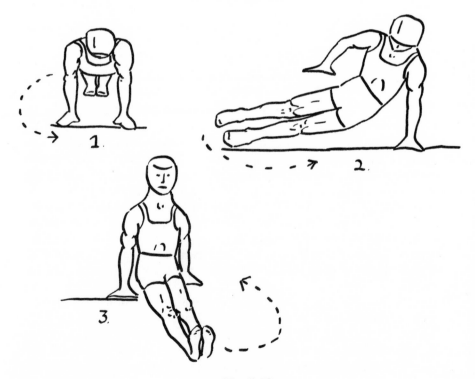

Fig. 5-30

*JUMP THRU*—Stand on one foot. Lift the other and hold it with the opposite hand in front of the foot. (The right hand holds the left foot or the left hand holds the right foot.) While holding the foot, jump over the held leg. Jump backward to the starting position. See Fig. 5-31.

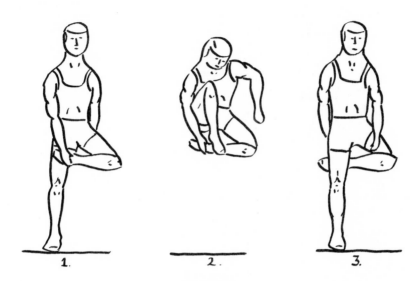

**Fig. 5-31**

*KANGAROO HOP*—Squat, keeping the legs together. Place the hands behind the neck. Jump forward on two feet for ten jumps without losing balance.

*JUMP TURN*—Straddle stand with one foot on either side of a tape line. Jump, and while in the air turn and land facing the opposite direction with the feet still straddling the line. Try one complete turn. See Fig. 5-32.

*KIP*—Back lying position. Lift the legs up and over the head into a pike position, parallel to the floor. Simultaneously snap the legs up and out while pushing with the hands and land in a squatting position on the mat. Recovery will be easier if the body leans forward at the conclusion of the stunt. See Fig. 5-33.

*SWEDISH FALL*—Standing position, arms at the sides. Fall forward, catching the body weight on the extended arms and hands, letting the elbows bend as the body is lowered to the floor. During the fall the correct body alignment between the feet and the head should be maintained. See Fig. 5-34.

## TEN ROLLS

*LOG ROLL*—Back lying position. Extend the arms overhead and keeping the legs straight and together roll sidewards in a straight line. The body should remain in alignment.

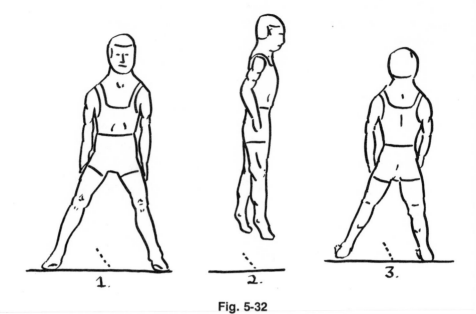

Fig. 5-32

Fig. 5-33

**Fig. 5-34**

*ROCKER*—Front lying position. Bend the legs at the knees and reach back with the arms and grasp the ankles. Pull hard on the ankles forcing the body to arch. Keep the head up. Rock forward and back on the chest and abdomen. See Fig. 5-35.

*CIRCLE ROLL*—Sit on the mat with the legs bent and the bottoms of the feet flat against each other. Grasp the ankles by reaching between the legs and under the ankles with the fingers on the outside of the legs. Let the body fall to the side and starting rolling in a circle from side to the back to side and up to a sit again. See Fig. 5-36.

*SHOULDER ROLL*—Stand with left foot slightly forward. Lean forward placing the hands on the mat. Continue to lean allowing the left arm to bend until the left shoulder touches the mat. Push off with the feet and roll to the left shoulder. Then continue the roll to the opposite hip and back to a standing position. If rolling over the right shoulder the right foot should be forward. See Fig. 5-37.

*FORWARD ROLL*—Squatting position with the hands on the mat shoulder width apart. Tuck the chin to the chest, lift the hips and roll forward onto the shoulders. Push off with the feet and continue the roll to a squat and then stand, keeping balance. See Fig. 5-38.

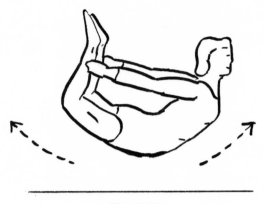

**Fig. 5-35**

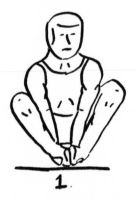

1.

2.

**Fig. 5-36**

**Fig. 5-37**

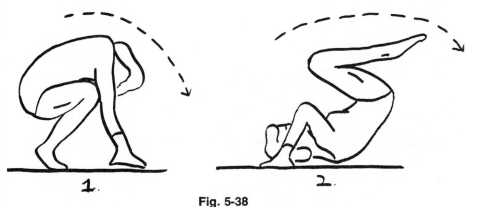

**Fig. 5-38**

*BACK SHOULDER ROLL*—Back lying position. Tuck the knees to the chest and start to roll backwards. As the weight is taken by the shoulders place the hands on the mat and turn the head slightly to one side so that the backward roll is done over one shoulder. Land on the knees. See Fig. 5-39.

**Fig. 5-39**

*BACKWARD ROLL*—Squatting position. Push off slightly and with the legs tucked to the chest roll back onto the back. As the shoulders touch the mat place the hands on the mat above the shoulders with the fingers pointing toward the shoulders. Continue to roll backward, tucking the head and pushing with the arms as the body goes over. Land in the squatting position. See Fig. 5-40.

*DIVE AND ROLL*—Standing position. Push off with the legs and lift the hips as in a jump but at the same time bend forward and place the hands on the mat, tuck the head, and roll forward onto the shoulders. See Fig. 5-41. As the roll is mastered place an obstacle, such as a rolled mat, which the performer must pass over in the air after the take-off and before the hands contact the mat for the roll.

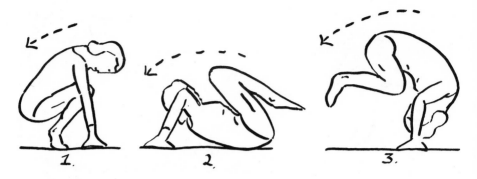

Fig. 5-40

Fig. 5-41

Fig. 5-42

*CARTWHEEL*—Standing position, feet slightly apart. Bend over and place the left hand on the mat to the left side of the body. Bend further and place the right hand on the mat on line with the left and keeping the arms straight, lift first the right leg and then the left overhead, passing through a momentary handstand and landing right foot and then left foot on line with, but on the other side of, the hands. The stunt is performed on line directly sideward from the starting position.

## WORKING WITH A PARTNER

*SIT AND STAND*—Two persons assume a long sitting position with their backs against each other. Then they interlock the arms at the elbows. Leaning backward slightly they both stand and then sit again without adjusting the arms or losing balance.

*WHEELBARROW*—One person assumes a push-up position on the floor. The other person picks up the legs of the first person and they walk—the first person on his hands, with the other holding the feet.

*FRONT SOMERSAULT*—The person assumes a stable standing position. The other person stands directly in front of the first and bends down and grasps her ankles. Then the person who is still standing picks up the legs of her partner and holds them at the ankles. She then bends forward and while holding the ankles of her partner does a forward roll through the legs of the other person. As the roll is completed, the person who had been upside down is now right side up and she does the next forward roll. Be sure not to let go of the ankles. See Fig. 5-42.

*CAMEL*—One person takes a stable standing position. The other places her hands on her partner's shoulders and wraps her legs around her partner's waist. Then keeping her legs in place, she lets go with her hands letting her body fall back until she can grasp the ankles of her partner. Then the person who had been standing bends over and places the hands on the floor. She then walks in this position. See Fig. 5-43.

**Fig. 5-43**

**Fig. 5-44**

**Fig. 5-44 (Continued)**

**Fig. 5-44 (Continued)**

Fig. 5-44 *(Continued)*

**Fig. 5-45**

**Fig. 5-45 (Continued)**

**Fig. 5-45 (Continued)**

**Fig. 5-45 *(Continued)***

**Fig. 5-46**

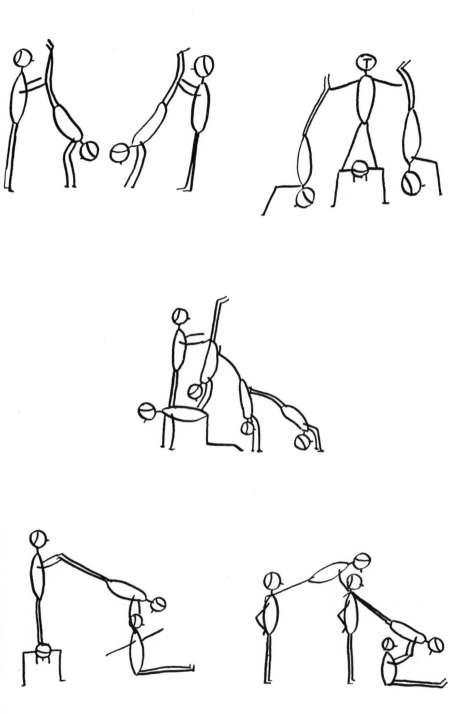

**Fig. 5-46** *(Continued)*

**Fig. 5-46** *(Continued)*

*PYRAMIDS*—These are balancing stunts designed for two, three, and four or more persons. The diagrams are easy to interpret, and therefore no individual directions are given. It is suggested that they be performed on mats, as students are likely to fall in the process of getting out of the pyramid at the end of the stunt. See Figs. 5-44, 5-45 and 5-46.

## FOR FURTHER REFERENCE

Fogel, S. J., *Gymnastics Handbook*. West Nyack, New York, Parker Publishing Company, Inc., 1971.

Orlick, E. and J. Mosley, *Teacher's Illustrated Handbook of Stunts*. Englewood Cliffs, Prentice-Hall, Inc., 1963.

Ryser, O. E., *A Manual for Tumbling and Apparatus Stunts*. Columbus, Brown, 1968.

Szypula, G., *Tumbling and Balancing for All*. Columbus, Brown, 1968.

# 6

# COMBINING ACTIVITIES—SETTING UP
# A CIRCUIT

The process of performing various exercises set up in a series is known as circuit training, one of the quickest and most effective ways to develop over-all physical conditioning. Because of its flexible nature, this type of training can be practiced almost anywhere, indoors or out, and with or without equipment. It adapts well to the classroom situation because it is easily supervised, can be done in a very short time, and can incorporate a large number of students at the same time. Circuits can be used for over-all conditioning or may be modified to work specific muscle groups which may need extra attention. Most importantly, circuit training activities can be "tailor made" for each individual student allowing maximum concentration on individual problems.

## PREPARING THE STUDENT

Setting up a circuit requires three preliminary activities. The first of these is teaching. It is necessary to instruct each student in the proper way to perform the given exercises for maximum benefit. The second is testing. Once the exercises are learned, the maximum performance level of each student must be found. This is done by having the individual perform as many repetitions of each exercise as he can in one minute. The last preliminary activity is timing. When the maximum level of performance for each exercise is known the circuit may be run. The student should be timed as he goes through the full circuit, performing half of his maximum level of exercises at each station. This timing is done three times on three different days.

After the timing the student is then ready to use the circuit for training. His objective is to reduce the amount of time required to complete the circuit, based on his average time from the three day timing sessions; or to increase the number of repetitions at each station, while keeping the over-all time for the circuit the same.

To help him keep track of his own performance, a training card, Fig. 6-1, is filled in with the names of the exercises, the number of repetitions to be performed (half his maximum performance), and his time. Each succeeding day he enters the number of repetitions of each exercise that he does, and the time the circuit took him to complete.

If he performs the circuit at the start of each class period he should be able to accomplish one or both of these goals. How long it will take depends upon the individual student.

Sample Circuit Training Card

| | Max. Perf. | Date | | | | | | |
|---|---|---|---|---|---|---|---|---|
| Name of Student | | | | | | | | |
| Date Begun | | | | | | | | |
| 1. Jump Rope | | | | | | | | |
| 2. Push-ups | | | | | | | | |
| 3. Step-ups on low bench | | | | | | | | |
| 4. Trunk lifts | | | | | | | | |
| 5. Bent knee sit-ups | | | | | | | | |
| 6. Shoulder stands | | | | | | | | |
| 7. Sit-ups & arches | | | | | | | | |
| 8. Split jumps | | | | | | | | |
| 9. Jumping jacks | | | | | | | | |
| Time | | | | | | | | |

**Fig. 6-1**

When setting up a circuit course there are several additional factors to consider:

1.  Select exercises that are simple to learn.
2.  Make sure that there are exercises to cover each major muscle group (unless the purpose of the circuit is to improve a specific muscle group).
3.  Try to set up the circuit in such a manner so that antagonistic muscle groups are worked alternately.
4.  Separate similar exercises by completely different ones working
    . different muscle groups.
5.  Start at a low performance level and work up slowly.

Once a circuit has been chosen various stations are set up around the class area. At each station is the name of the exercise and a description, with a diagram if possible, of how it should be done. At the start the students can go to any of the stations, thus spreading out the group. Then each student does each exercise according to the number of repetitions listed in his own program.

## SAMPLE CIRCUITS

In the following examples the reader should refer to the Index for the location of the descriptions of any unfamiliar exercises.

### CIRCUIT A–GENERAL CONDITIONING

(No equipment needed.)
1.  Jumping Jacks
2.  Half Squats
3.  Prone Leg Lifts
4.  Bent Knee Sit-ups
5.  Push-ups
6.  Bridge
7.  Squares
8.  Sprinter

### CIRCUIT B–GENERAL CONDITIONING

(No equipment needed.)
1.  Jumping Jacks
2.  Squat Thrusts

3. Run Laps
4. Push-ups
5. Prone Leg Lifts
6. Run Laps
7. Bent Knee Sit-ups
8. Lunges
9. Run Laps

## CIRCUIT C–GENERAL CONDITIONING

(Equipment needed—one short jump rope, one low bench approximately twelve inches high.)
1. Jump Rope
2. Push-ups
3. Step-ups on the Bench
4. Trunk Lifts
5. Bent Knee Sit-ups
6. Shoulder Stands
7. Sit-ups and Arches
8. Split Jumps
9. Jumping Jacks

## CIRCUIT D–GENERAL CONDITIONING

(Equipment needed—One short jump rope, one medicine ball, one low bench, one wand.)
1. Jump Rope
2. Medicine Ball Toss
3. Step-ups on the Bench
4. Sit-ups
5. Push-ups with Feet Support on the Bench
6. Jump Through the Wand
7. Run Laps

## CIRCUIT E–UPPER BODY CONDITIONING

(No equipment needed.)
1. Push-ups
2. Bridge
3. Wing Stretcher
4. Shoulder Curls
5. Shoulder Stretch
6. Up Oars
7. Arm Circles
8. Push-ups with Arms and Hands on Line with Head.

## CIRCUIT F–LOWER BODY CONDITIONING

(Equipment needed—one short jump rope, low bench.)
1. Jump Rope
2. Squat Thrusts
3. Body Bends
4. Step-ups on Low Bench
5. Leg Raises
6. Split Jumps
7. Sprinter

## FARTLEK—USING THE OUT-OF-DOORS

Fartlek, or Speed-play, originated in Sweden in the late 1940's. The basic principle of Fartlek training is that of alternating long paced runs, jogs, sprints, and rhythmic exercises while traveling over a course of varied terrain. This type of training may be practiced in a park, on a beach, in the snow, over hills or almost anywhere at anytime. Ideally, the course should include several hills, flat stretches and other terrain variations. It is through this kind of undulating course that all the muscle groups used in running are strengthened.

There are several advantages to Fartlek. First of all it develops self-reliance because the individual is often on his own while training. It presents a mental and physical challenge yet at the same time is refreshing because of the varied training surface. It develops the kind of endurance necessary for almost any kind of endurance activity. It also allows the individual to do a great deal of work without realizing it. Lastly, it can be practiced anywhere, day or night, winter or summer.

A typical Fartlek course might start by jogging very slowly for about five minutes to serve as a warm-up; then run at a faster pace for one half to one minute; jog until normal breath rate has been recovered; ten jumping jacks; jog two mintues; ten trunk twists; alternate sprints and jogs for five to ten minutes; ten toe touches; run hard for about 200 yards; and jog slowly to cool down.

To vary the Fartlek course it may include uphill sprints, striding down hills, running hills on the diagonal, weaving in and out between trees, or anything else the runner may feel inclined to do.

Another very important part of Fartlek training is the inclusion of bending, stretching, twisting, circling and flexing exercises. In this manner the student can maintain a loose relaxed state while recovering from a hard run and at the same time help to tone muscle groups other than those used in running.

Some Fartlek variations are as follows:

1. *INDIAN FILE*—Students start in single file five to ten yards apart. This distance depends on the size of the group. Everyone starts to jog in a single file. The last man must sprint to the front of the line while doing one of the following:
   a. As he passes the runners the man running must call out each person's name. Failure to do this sends the runner back to the end of the line.
   b. As he sprints to the front, he must weave in and out of the line.
   c. Two of the end runners start together, one on each side of the line and race to the front. The loser must return to the rear.

2. *FOX AND HOUNDS*—Choose from the group one to three students to be the foxes and give them a head start of ten to thirty seconds. The rest of the group are the hounds. They must chase the foxes until all the foxes are caught. Make sure the course has a boundary and is not laid out in a straight line. To vary the activity:
   a. Time each fox to see which one can stay free the longest.
   b. Set up teams, one being the foxes and the other the hounds. After all the foxes are caught switch roles. See which group of foxes can stay free the longest.

## FOR FURTHER REFERENCE

Doherty, J. K., *Modern Training for Running.* Englewood Cliffs, Prentice-Hall, Inc., 1964.

Klafs, C. E., and D. D. Arnheim, *Modern Principles of Athletic Training.* St. Louis, Mosby, 1973.

Morgan, R. E., and G. T. Adamson, *Circuit Training.* New Rochelle, New York, Soccer Associates, 1961.

Rosandich, Ward, and Lawson, *The American Training Pattern.* Upson, Wisconsin, Olympia, n.d.

Wilt, F. ed., *Track Technique.* Los Altos, California.

# 7

# SKIPPING ROPE FOR DEVELOPING COORDINATION

The jump rope, once a child's toy, is now a valuable aid in the development of coordination for the more mature high school student. What was a fun pastime has become a challenging training activity. Rope jumping first of all builds strength, both in the arm and leg muscles and in the cardiovascular system. The variety of possibilities in footwork while jumping aids the development of balance, while the continuous action aspect of the activity promotes endurance. Coordination develops as these factors are combined to form challenging jumping routines.

The activities in this chapter are divided into four groups. It begins with solo jumping where one jumper works with one rope. The rope itself should be long enough to reach from the floor in its center, up to the shoulders with the ends. In schools where a variety of children will use one rope the average length should be about nine to ten feet. Any excess rope can be wound around the wrists of the performer. When turning the rope for solo jumping the main action is in the wrists, which should be relaxed. Though there is some elbow movement, they too should be relaxed and in, close to the body. Shoulder action is very slight. When jumping the body should be pushed up and off the floor rather than having just the knees bend to let the rope pass under the body.

The second group of activities use a long rope with one person at either end to work the rope for the jumper. This requires a rope of from fifteen to twenty feet in length. Again the turning action should be made with relaxed elbows and wrists.

The last two sections contain stunts using two ropes and partner activities. These are more complicated and should be attempted only after the student can solo jump and use the long rope successfully.

## SOLO JUMPING

The performer has one rope, the ends of which he holds in each hand, and he turns it himself.

1. Swing the rope forward and backward, stepping over it as it passes under the body. The rope does not pass over the head.
2. Swing the rope forward and backward and jump over it as it passes under the body.
3. Swing the rope backward, over the head and down in front of the body. Step over it as it comes toward the feet.
4. Swing the rope backward, over the head and down in front of the body. Jump over it as it comes toward the feet.
5. Jump over the rope and make a second, smaller jump as the rope passes overhead.
6. Jump in place, first on one foot and then on the other.
7. Jump, turning the rope in the other direction, backward.
8. Jump, turning the rope with the arms crossed in front of the body. Extend the arms as far as possible in the cross.
9. Run forward while turning the rope.
10. Jump, turning in a circle while jumping.
11. Jump once in the regular manner and jump a second time with the arms crossed in front of the body. Continue on an alternating basis.
12. Jump on one foot and keep the other leg extended in front of the body.
13. Jump on alternate feet, extending the lifted leg in front of the body by swinging it forward after each jump.
14. Clap hands or hit the rope handles together each time the rope is jumped.
15. Between jumps swing the rope in a circle to the right and then left of the body making a figure eight.
16. Between jumps, circle the rope overhead.
17. Shorten the rope and jump in a squat position.
18. Cross the feet when landing and uncross and extend the legs while in the air.
19. Jump twice to each turn of the rope.

20. Jump, landing alternately with the feet in a side-stride position and then together.
21. Jump, landing alternately with the feet together and parallel and then with the feet crossed.
22. Jump alternately with the feet and arms crossed and feet and arms apart.
23. Run, taking two steps between each jump.
24. Run, and as the rope turns, leap over it, taking two running steps between each leap.
25. Jump over the rope with one foot, hop on that foot and then repeat with the other foot, thus doing a skipping pattern.
26. Gallop using the rope.
27. Jump pepper, turning the rope as fast as possible while continuing to jump.
28. Increase the difficulty by performing the above steps in an increasing number of repetitions.
29. Combine several of the steps in specified repetitions to form a routine.
30. Perform one jump or routine for a specified time period.

## SKIPPING THE LONG ROPE

With the rope held stationary by one person at either end, and with the majority of the length of the rope resting on the floor:

Jump the rope and continue to jump over it. However, before each jump the people holding the rope should raise it slightly. As it gets higher off the ground a running start may be necessary.

With the rope held stationary by one person at either end and at a height even with the performer's knees:

1. Stand on one side of the rope and step over it to the other side.
2. Stand on one side and jump over it landing on two feet.
3. Jump over the rope and while in the air make a half turn and land facing the rope.
4. Jump over the rope and while in the air make a full turn and land facing away from the rope.
5. Jump over the rope and while in the air tuck the legs and touch the toes.
6. Jump over and while in the air split the legs out sideward and touch the toes without bending the knees.
7. Jump the rope with one leg going over first and the other leg following.
8. Dive and roll over the rope, using mats to cushion the landing area.
9. Jump over the rope and while in the air tap the heels together.
10. Try the above stunts with the rope slightly higher.

With the rope being turned by a person at either end:

1. Swing the rope back and forth without circling it overhead. Stand next to the rope and jump as it approaches.
2. Gradually increase the back and forth swing until the rope circles over the head. Continue jumping.
3. Run through the turning rope without letting it touch the body.
4. Run in the "front door," moving in the same direction as the rope is turning, jump, and then run out the "back door," or the other side.
5. Run in the "back door," moving in the opposite direction that the rope is turning, jump, and run out the "front door."
6. Run in, jump a specified number of times and run out.
7. Touch the ground at specified intervals while jumping.
8. Bounce a ball while jumping.
9. Jump with the hands and feet on the ground, placing the hands and then the feet over the rope. The performer should stand at right angles to those turning the rope.
10. Jump and perform the tuck, split, or toe touch jumps.
11. Jump pepper, having those turning the rope turn it as fast as possible.
12. Jump and make a half turn on each landing.
13. Perform jumping exercises (Chapters 2 and 3) while jumping.

## USING TWO ROPES

With two turners having one end of a long rope in each hand:

1. Turn double Dutch. The ropes are turned alternately toward each other.
2. Turn double Irish. The two ropes are turned alternately away from each other.
3. Turn egg beater. Add two more turners and position them so that the two ropes are at right angles to each other.

*Note:* With several ropes and several turners it is necessary to stress coordination of effort on the part of the turners in order to establish a good rhythm. With two persons turning the long rope the jumper can try to jump with his own individual rope doing the solo jumping stunts at the same time he is jumping the long rope.

## PARTNER SKILLS

With a short rope held by one person in the solo jumping position:

1. Partners jump facing each other.

2.  Non-turning partner faces away from the turner.
3.  Partner runs in, jumps, and runs out again while the other person is jumping.
4.  Non-turning partner touches the floor between jumps.
5.  Non-turning partner turns in a circle as he jumps.
6.  Both persons turn the rope with the right hand and place their left hand on their partner's shoulder.
7.  Jump pepper together.

With the rope held by one hand of each person, with the jumpers standing side by side:

1.  Face the same direction and place inside arms around each other's waist. Outside hands turn the rope. Perform solo jumping stunts.
2.  Face opposite directions. Turn with the outside hands and place the other hands on partner's shoulders or link elbows. Perform solo jumping stunts.

Using the long rope or ropes:

1.  Run in with partner, holding hands.
2.  See how many jumpers can singly enter the rope, jump together and leave.
3.  Jump with a partner and change places while jumping.
4.  Perform long rope stunts together.
5.  Run in, turn, face partner who is outside the rope. Catch a ball thrown by the partner and then throw it back.
6.  Both partners run in and play catch, bouncing or throwing the ball to each other.
7.  Play "follow the leader" while jumping.

# 8

# ACTIVITIES USING HAND APPARATUS

Once the uncoordinated student begins to gain some control over purposeful movement of his body it is time to introduce activities involving other moving objects. This will aid the student in developing two of the more complex areas of coordination. The first is the coordination between the hands and the eyes. In most instances, it is the hands which give impetus to the object which the eyes must then track. In order for the bodily movement to be coordinated in relationship to the moving object (the second aspect of coordination to be emphasized) this tracking and its mental image need to be quite accurate. Activities using small hand apparatus will help the student to improve his hand-eye coordination and his mental integration of this perceptual information.

This hand apparatus includes small balls (eight inches in diameter or smaller), hoops (the plastic variety similar to Hula Hoops), Indian pins, and wooden wands. For some of the activities the teacher might want to substitute tires, both bicycle and car type, for the hoops. Plastic tubes, such as the ones used in golf bags could be substituted for wands, and bean bags could be used for many of the ball handling activities. There should be enough equipment so that each student can have his own piece of apparatus. In addition to the activities listed here, which are listed in an approximate order of difficulty within each section, the student should be encouraged to experiment with the equipment, developing both additional exercises and original routines on his own.

## HOOPS

1. Roll the hoop and walk along side.
2. Roll the hoop and run along side.
3. Roll the hoop along a straight tape line on the floor and run along side.
4. Roll the hoop away from the body and then run through the hoop while it is rolling.
5. Hold the hoop waist high and parallel to the ground with the hands close together in front of the body. Keeping the hands in place, let the other side of the hoop swing down. Jump into the hoop as it nears the floor and let it continue to swing upward until it is again parallel to the floor. Then reverse the swing of the hoop, jump out of it and let it swing up to its original position. See Fig. 8-1.

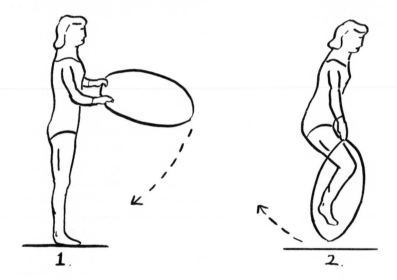

**Fig. 8-1**

6. Place the hoop around the waist. Rotate the hips, letting the hoop swing around the body like a Hula Hoop.
7. Hold one arm sideward and parallel to the floor at shoulder level. Hang the hoop on the upper arm. Rotate the arm until the hoop swings around the arm.
8. Lift one leg off the floor and hang the hoop from the knee. Rotate the leg from the hip joint until the hoop swings around and around the leg. See Fig. 8-2.
9. Stand with the feet together. Place the hoop around the knees. By rotating the body, with the feet as the axis, spin the hoop around the knees. See Fig. 8-3.

**Fig. 8-2**

**Fig. 8-3**

10. Start the hoop rotating around the waist. Then, by changing the point of rotation, move the hoop up and down the body as it spins. See Fig. 8-4.
11. Hold the hoop next to the side of the body with its lower edge resting on the floor. Swing the lower edge toward the body and jump sideward into the hoop. Let it swing back down and jump out again.
12. Hold the hoop in front of the body with two hands which are approximately a foot apart. Use the hoop like a jump rope, letting it swing down

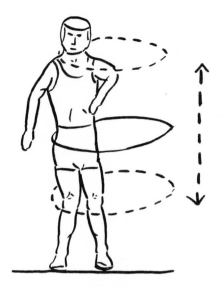

**Fig. 8-4**

jumping in, letting one edge lift up backward and over the head and down in front of the body.

13.  Once it can be used like a jump rope try some of the solo jumping stunts from Chapter 7.

14.  Hold the hoop in front of the body, and perpendicular to it. Step over the lower edge of the hoop and through it with the left leg. Then, with the right leg step across in front of the left one and across and into the hoop. Continue crossing one foot over the other letting the legs remain in the hoop. Roll the hoop forward while walking. See Fig. 8-5.

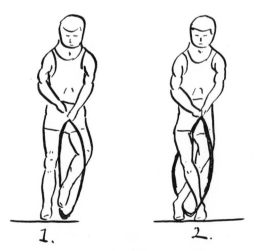

**Fig. 8-5**

15. Hold the hoop in front of the body parallel to the floor. Step into the hoop with one foot. Lift the hoop up on one side so that one edge passes over the head and down the other side of the body. See Fig. 8-6. Lift the other leg and free the hoop.

**Fig. 8-6**

16. Using a hoop with a diameter no greater than two feet, lay the hoop on the ground. Step into the hoop and start by hooking one edge of the hoop over the toes. Then, by exerting varying sideward pressure against the hoop with the legs, work the hoop up the body.

## INDIAN PINS

1. Straddle stand position. Hold the small end of one pin in each hand. Move the arms from the shoulder in as large a circle as possible. Try to keep the arms straight. See Fig. 8-7.
2. Straddle stand position. Hold the small end of one pin in each hand with the arms lifted sideward at shoulder level. Let both arms swing down, crossing in front of the body. Then as they swing back lift the arms back to shoulder level.
3. Straddle stand position. Hold the pin by the small end with the pin parallel to the ground and the other end pointing away from the body. With gentle wrist action flip the pin over toward the body and catch the large end. Repeat and catch the small end.

**Fig. 8-7**

*Variation:*
a. Toss with one hand and catch with the other.
b. Toss it in a complete circle, holding and catching only with the small end.
4. Straddle stand position. Hold the pin with both hands extended toward the floor in front of the body. Keeping the arms relatively straight, rotate the trunk from the waist moving the pin in as large a circle as possible.

## SMALL BALLS

1. Bounce and catch it with two hands.
2. Bounce and catch it with the eyes closed.
3. Bounce it repeatedly with one hand.
4. Bounce it repeatedly with one hand and the eyes closed.
5. Bounce it first with one hand and then the other on an alternating basis.
6. Keeping the feet stationary, bounce the ball in a circle around the body.
7. Bounce the ball in a figure eight pattern around the legs. See Fig. 8-8.
8. Bounce the ball and turn in a complete circle before catching it.
9. Hold the ball at waist level against the body. Roll it in a complete circle around the body. See Fig. 8-9.
   *Variation:*
   Progress up and down the body as the ball goes around it.
10. Bounce the ball and see how many times the hands can be clapped before catching it.
11. Toss the ball into the air and catch it with both hands.
12. Toss it with one hand and catch it with one hand.

**Fig. 8-8**

**Fig. 8-9**

13. Toss it into the air with one hand and catch it with the other.
14. Hold the ball in one hand with the palm of the hand under the ball. Lift the arm sideward and toss the ball in an arc over the head and catch it with the other hand on the other side of the body. See Fig. 8-10.
15. Toss the ball into the air and turn around in a circle before catching it.
16. In a long sitting position, holding the ball in both hands:
    a. Lean forwards and place the ball between the ankles.
    b. Lean backward and lie on the back, lifting the legs with the ball between the ankles.

**Fig. 8-10**

    c. Take the ball with the hands and place it on the floor over the head.
    d. Pike the legs over the head and pick up the ball with the ankles. See Fig. 8-11.
    e. Lift the feet toward the ceiling.
    f. Take the ball back with the hands.
    g. Lower the legs.
    h. Return to a long sit.

17. Lie on the floor on the back. Toss the ball toward the ceiling and catch it before it hits the ground.
18. In a back lying position toss the ball up with one hand and catch it with the other.
19. In a back lying position toss the ball up and clap hands before catching it.
20. Assume a back lying position with the soles of the feet against a wall and the legs straight. Toss the ball against the wall and catch it before it touches the body or the floor.
21. In a back lying position with the feet against the wall toss the ball against the wall and roll sideward one complete roll before catching it. See Fig. 8-12.
22. Bounce the ball with the left hand and as the ball hits the floor, lift the right leg and pass the leg over the ball, moving the leg sideward to the right. Repeat on the opposite side. See Fig. 8-13.

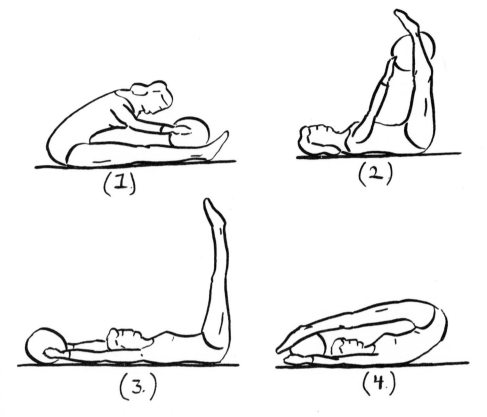

Fig. 8-11

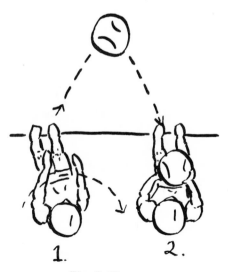

Fig. 8-12

**Fig. 8-13**

23. Toss the ball against a wall and catch it on one bounce.
24. Toss the ball against a wall and catch it before it bounces.
25. Toss the ball against a wall and turn around in a complete circle before catching the ball either on one bounce or before it hits the ground.
26. Lift the right leg. Holding the ball in the right hand, toss it under the right leg and against the wall. Catch it before it hits the ground. Repeat to the other side. See Fig. 8-14.

**Fig. 8-14**

27. Bounce the ball and hit it with the palm of an open hand. Hit it so that it hits a wall without bouncing and catch it before it hits the floor.
28. Alternate bouncing and catching stunts with tossing and catching stunts.
29. Hold the ball behind the hips with two hands. Toss it up behind the head and over it. Catch the ball in front of the body. See Fig. 8-15.

**Fig. 8-15**

## WANDS

The following wand activities are designed to be performed by one person working alone.

1. Straddle standing position, holding a wand as high as possible above the head and parallel to the ground with one hand at either end. Keeping the legs straight, bend forward and attempt to touch the wand to the floor. Return to a stand with the wand lifted.
2. Straddle stand with the wand held parallel to the floor at shoulder level. The arms should be lifted forward with the elbows straight, and one hand on each end of the wand. Keeping the arms straight and the wand parallel to the floor, twist the trunk as far as possible to the right and then as far as possible to the left. Let the arms lead the twisting action. See Fig. 8-16.
3. Straddle stand with the wand held perpendicular to the floor by one hand grasping it at the middle. Toss the wand into the air and catch it again.
   *Variation:*
   a. Toss it with one hand and catch it with the other.
   b. Toss the wand sideward across the front of the body and catch it with the other hand.

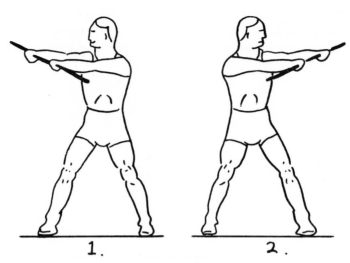

**Fig. 8-16**

4. Back lying position with the arms extended overhead along the floor holding the wand at each end. Sit up, and keeping the legs straight lower the wand forward and touch it to the floor on the other side of the soles of the feet. Lift the wand and return to the back lying position. See Fig. 8-17.

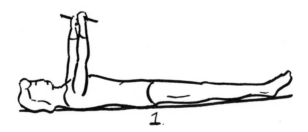

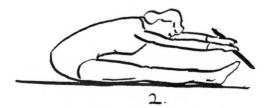

**Fig. 8-17**

5. Straddle stand with the wand held parallel to the floor at shoulder level. The arms should be lifted forward with the elbows straight and one hand on each end of the wand. Keeping hold of the ends of the wand, cross the arms, turning the wand over. Simultaneously bend forward and after the wand is turned touch it to the floor. Return to the standing position and uncross the arms, returning to the starting position. Be sure to keep the knees straight while bending forward. See Fig. 8-18.

**Fig. 8-18**

6. Hold the wand in front of the body with the palms of the hands under the wand holding it parallel to the floor. Toss it into the air in this parallel position and catch it again with both hands.
   *Variation:*
   a. Toss and catch it with one hand.
   b. Toss it with one hand and catch it with the other.
7. Straddle stand, holding one wand in each hand. Grasp the wands in the center and hold them parallel to the ground at shoulder level on either side of the body. Turn the wands over by turning the wrists. Then turn them back to the starting position. Keep the elbows extended.
8. Straddle stand. Hold the wand with both hands in front of the body. Lift it over the head and lower it behind the back. Return to the front position. Do not let go of the wand. See Fig. 8-19.

The following wand activities are designed to be performed by partners sharing wands.

1. Assume a long sit position with the bottoms of the feet flat against the partner's and the legs straight. With both people grasping one wand with

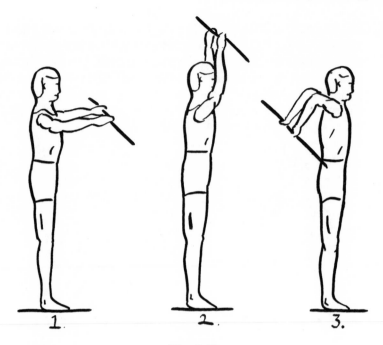

**Fig. 8-19**

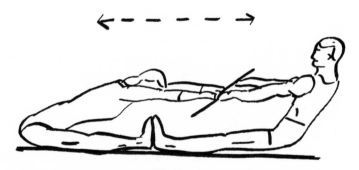

**Fig. 8-20**

the hands shoulder width apart, one person leans back towards the floor as the other person leans forward. Then reverse the action. Lean as far as possible in the direction of movement. See Fig. 8-20.

2.  Standing position, one behind the other, with the end of one wand held in each hand and the other end held in the corresponding hand of the partner. Keeping the arms straight, lift the wands overhead and then lower them back down to the side.

*Variation:*

At the same time the arms are lifted, jump to a straddle. Jump and close the feet as the arms are lowered.

3. Standing position, one behind the other, with the end of one wand held in each hand and the other end held in the corresponding hand of the partner. Bend the elbows and bring the wands up to the shoulders. Push them straight overhead and then lower them slowly back down to the sides. See Fig. 8-21.

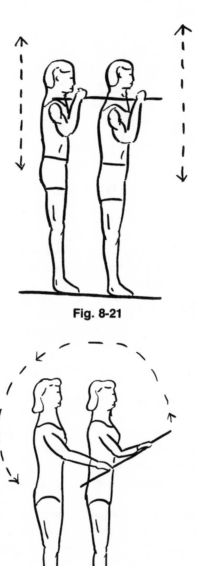

**Fig. 8-21**

**Fig. 8-22**

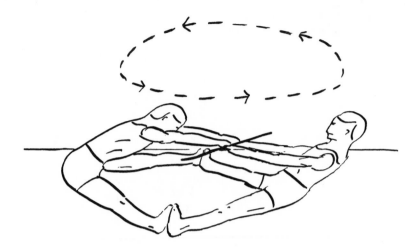

**Fig. 8-23**

4.  Standing position, one behind the other, with the end of one wand held in each hand and the other end held in the corresponding hand of the partner. Swing the arms forward up into the air and around behind the body, back down to the sides, making a complete circle. See Fig. 8-22.
5.  Long sitting position facing each other. Spread the legs with the soles of the feet touching. Each partner holds the wand with both hands. Keeping the seat on the floor they move the wand in as large a circle as possible. See Fig. 8-23.

## FOR FURTHER REFERENCE

Bednar, C., *Sokol Gymnastic Manual*. Perth Amboy, New Jersey, Slovak Gymnastic Union, 1956.

Drury, Blanche, and A. Schmid, *Gymnastics for Women*. Palo Alto, National, 1966.

Edgar, K., "Hand Apparatus," *Gymnastic Guide*. Washington, American Association for Health, Physical Education and Recreation, 1965.

Prchal, M., *Gymnastique Moderne*. Tucson, United States Gymnastic Federation, 1969.

Provaznik and Zabka, *Gymnastic Activities With Hand Apparatus*. Minneapolis, Burgess, 1966.

# 9

# DEVELOPING COORDINATION
# WITH THE TRAMPOLINE

The force of gravity tends to restrict human movement to that which can be accomplished on or in close proximity to the ground. Movements performed while off the ground and in the air are quite limited and of short duration. The trampoline provides a means of overcoming the force of gravity for slightly longer periods of time, during which a variety of activities can be performed. As these activities are executed under entirely new conditions, they provide an additional means of developing coordination unlike any other.

Before considering the variety of activities possible, it is important to consider the safety percautions necessary when using this piece of equipment. Though the trampoline is not an essentially dangerous piece of apparatus, there are several factors which should be accounted for, particularily since the students for whom these activities are designed are below average in over-all ability. The trampoline itself should have a full size bed (6' × 12'). Junior trampolines are suitable for younger, smaller children. It should have a frame whose parts do not extend under the bed itself. The springs and frame should be covered with frame pads to prevent injury should someone land on them. The bed can be made of canvas or nylon. (Though canvas is cheaper it usually takes more weight to get a higher bounce.) Both a spotting belt for spotting from the floor as well as an overhead spotting apparatus are important. Diagrams of the various safety attachments are available upon request from trampoline dealers.

Once suitable equipment has been obtained students need to be aware of the precautions which they must take to insure safety. When not in use, such as between classes, the tramp should be half folded to discourage unsupervised use. During class it should only be used when the instructor is in the room. Every performer needs to be spotted and this can be accomplished in several ways. The easiest is to station other class members around the tramp, at least four, one on each side, and more than four if at all possible. Their job is to watch the performer, tell him if he is moving off center and push him back onto the bed should he start to bounce or fall off. Another method of spotting involves using the spotting belt and an overhead suspension system. The performer wears the belt, and the ropes which are attached to it run up to the ceiling and over to one side where they are controlled by one person, usually the instructor or a capable assistant. This reduces the need for other people around the bed while providing greater control of the uncoordinated performer who might have a great deal of trouble controlling his bouncing.

The most important part of trampoline safety is the responsibility of the performer. He should wear clothes which are easy to move in with no loose ties or belts. Bare feet can cause toes to get caught in the webbing so socks or gymnastic shoes should be worn. Tennis shoes hamper the "feel" for the bed and thus are not recommended. The student needs to follow the advice of his teacher and try only those activities which the teacher feels the student is ready to perform. The activities listed here are arranged in ascending order of difficulty. Though students may progress at different rates they should all follow the same general sequence in order to improve their over-all balance and strength as well as coordination.

## STUNTS ON THE BED

CRAWL—Get onto the bed at one of the ends (always have students get on at one end and off at the other to avoid collisions), crawl to the other end, and then sit on the edge of the frame and slide off feet first. See Fig. 9-1. Instruct students that they should always get down from the sitting position. Do not jump off.

LOG ROLL—Get on at the end and lie across the bed, parallel to the end. Extend the arms and legs and roll in a straight line to the other end. Dismount.

SEAL WALK—Mount, lie on the stomach lengthwise on the bed. Place the hands under the shoulders and push up until the arms are straight. Walk on the hands, letting the legs and lower trunk drag. Dismount at the other end.

MOUNT DISMOUNT

**Fig. 9-1**

*EGG ROLL*—Mount. Lie across the bed parallel to the end. Bring the knees to the chest and wrap the arms around them. Roll sideward to the other end. The head should not touch the bed. Dismount.

*SHOULDER ROLL*—Mount. Lie on the back, lengthwise on the bed. Tuck the knees to the chest, extend the legs overhead and roll backward over one shoulder, turning the head out to the other side. Finish on the knees. If space permits, repeat the stunt. Dismount.

*FORWARD ROLL*—Mount. Squat at one end facing the other end. Place the hands on the bed, tuck the head down, lift the seat and roll forward. Finish seated. Repeat if space permits. Dismount.

*BACKWARD ROLL*—Mount. Squat facing the near end of the tramp. Remain tucked as a roll backward is executed. To finish the roll place the hands over the shoulders onto the bed and push to allow the head room to clear as the roll is completed. Finish on the knees. Repeat if space permits. Dismount.

*V SEAT*—Mount. Crawl to the exact center of the tramp. (It may already be marked in the webbing. If not, a large ''+'' can be placed on the area with tape.) Sit in the center, facing the end. Extend the arms out to the side, lift the legs straight up off the bed till the body forms a V. Keeping the legs straight and together hold this position for ten seconds. Crawl to the end and dismount.

*ANGEL BALANCE*—Mount. Move to the center. Assume a hands and knees position. Extend one arm forward and the opposite leg backward. Lift head and hold for ten seconds. Repeat using the other arm and leg. Dismount.

*SHOULDER STAND*—Mount and move to the center. Lie flat on the back and lift the legs toward the ceiling, balancing on the shoulders and keeping the hips off the floor. Hold for ten seconds. Lower the legs and dismount.

*TIP-UP*—Mount. Move to the center. Place the hands and forehead in a triangular pattern on the bed. Take the support of the body on the hands and head (at approximately the front hairline) while placing the knees on the elbows. Hold for ten seconds. Dismount.

*HEAD STAND*—Mount. Assume the tip-up position in the center of the bed. Extend the legs toward the ceiling into a head stand. Hold for ten seconds. Recover and dismount.

*STAND*—Mount. Move to the center. Stand up and remain standing motionless for ten seconds. Get back down on the bed, and crawl to the end. Dismount.

*WALK*—Mount. Stand and walk to the center of the bed. Stop and stand for ten seconds. Walk to the other end. Sit down and dismount.

## BOUNCING STUNTS

Henceforth, it is assumed that the student will mount the tramp at one end and walk to the center and stop, before each stunt is begun. At the conclusion of the stunt the performer should stop, walk to the other end, sit down and dismount feet first, holding the frame for support. In addition, for most stunts two or three preliminary bounces are necessary to do the stunt and recover properly. Students should limit their time on the tramp to approximately ten bounces per turn. This helps to avoid fatigue and gives everyone plenty of practice time.

*BASIC BOUNCE AND STOP*—From a stand with the feet shoulder width apart, bend the knees and push off upward as if to jump in place. Continue bouncing lightly, attempting to remain on the center spot. To stop or "kill" the bounce, as the landing is made bend the knees and keep them bent rather than pushing off again. (This method for stopping should be used at the conclusion of each series of stunts.) See Fig. 9-2.

*BOUNCE WITH ARM LIFT*—With each bounce, as the body lifts into the air the arms are lifted forward and up over the shoulders in the start of a circle. As the body comes down the arms complete the circle moving back and down. In addition, as the arm action becomes synchronized with the bounce the arms can be used to aid in the lift. See Fig. 9-3.

*LEG CLOSE*—The basic bounce and arm lift are performed. As the arms lift, the legs close in the air and the toes are pointed. As the landing is made the legs are spread and the performer lands with the feet shoulder width apart.

*TUCK JUMP*—After a few preliminary bounces (necessary for all jumps and drops), while in the air, the knees are brought up to the chest and the arms wrap around the knees. Then the tuck is released and the performer lands as in a regular bounce.

*SPLIT JUMP*—While in the air the legs assume a split position and the arms

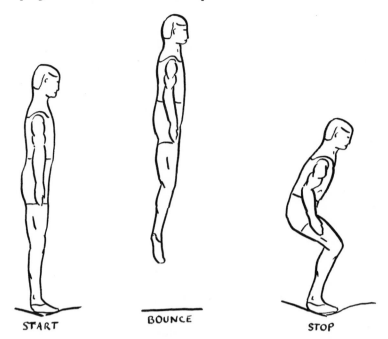

START            BOUNCE           STOP

**Fig. 9-2**

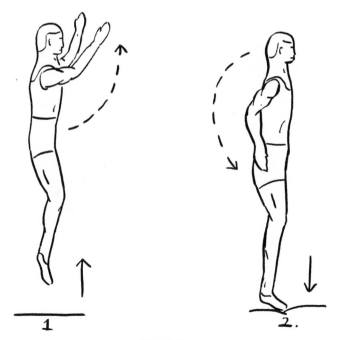

1            2.

**Fig. 9-3**

**Fig. 9-4**

correspond to the legs in an outward spread position. The performer should try both a side split and a forward/backward split. See Fig. 9-4.

*STAG JUMP*—While in the air the right arm and leg are extended to the right side. The left foot is brought pointed to the right knee and the left arm reaches horizontally across the front of the body parallel to the right arm. The jump is then repeated to the other side. See Fig. 9-5.

**Fig. 9-5**

*JUMP TURN*—While in the air make one quarter turn and land facing the side of the tramp. See Fig. 9-6. Continue turning one quarter on each jump until the original position is reached. Repeat going in the opposite direction. Perform with half turns. Try three quarter and full turns only if and when shorter turns can be done with control.

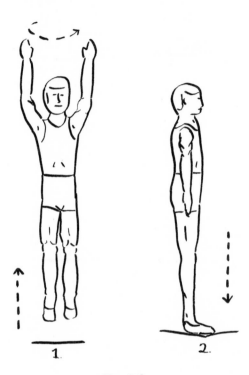

**Fig. 9-6**

*SEAT DROP*—Land in the long sit position, hands on the bed next to the seat. As the body leaves the bed tuck and stand on the next bounce. See Fig. 9-7.

*KNEE DROP*—Land on both knees and return to a stand on the next bounce. The body should be kept in alignment from the knees through the head. See Fig. 9-8.

*HANDS AND KNEES DROP*—Land on both knees and both hands and return to a stand on the next bounce. See Fig. 9-9.

*BACK DROP*—Begin in a squatting position on the bed (no preliminary bounces until the drop position is learned). Grasp the knees, tuck the chin forward and gently rock backwards landing on the shoulders and back. See Fig. 9-10. Lean forwards to return to the squatting position on the next bounce. When proficiency in this skill has been developed, gradually attempt the stunt from positions graduating from a squat to a stand. Add the preliminary bounces only when the performer can perform the stunt from a stand.

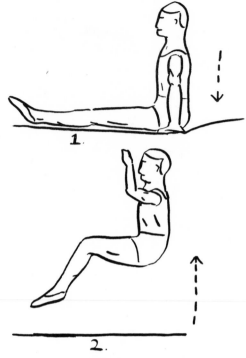

**Fig. 9-7**

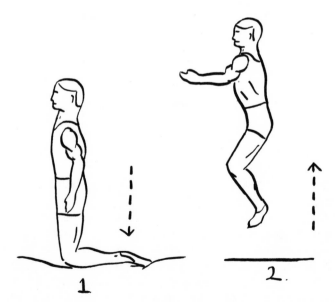

**Fig. 9-8**

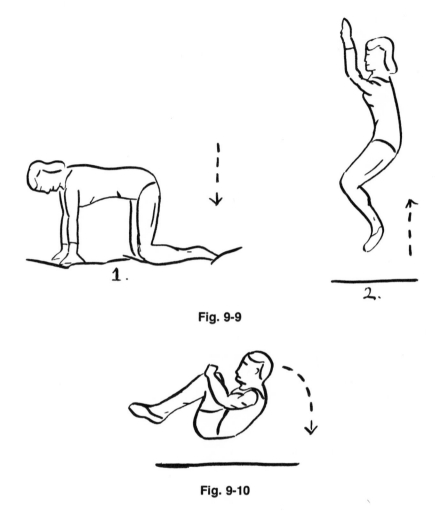

**Fig. 9-9**

**Fig. 9-10**

*FRONT DROP*—In the learning stage this stunt should be performed from a knee drop to lessen the chance of injury due to inaccurate positioning. Landing is on the front of the body, legs together and extended, toes pointed, hands flat on the mat under the shoulders. Return to a stand on the next bounce. See Fig. 9-11.

## BOUNCE COMBINATIONS

Each combination should be initiated with two or three preliminary bounces. They are listed in ascending order of difficulty. The more stunts required in the combination, the greater the difficulty both in endurance and coordination.

**Fig. 9-11**

## TWO STUNTS

Tuck jump, split jump. See Fig. 9-12.
Split jump, stag jump.
Tuck jump, stag jump.
Half turn, tuck jump.
Split jump, half turn.
Stag jump, half turn.
Knee drop, seat drop.
Tuck jump, knee drop.
Knee drop, split jump.
Stag jump, knee drop.
Knee drop, half turn.
Knee drop, hands and knees drop.
Hands and knees drop, split jump.
Stag jump, hands and knees drop.
Knee drop, front drop.
Hands and knees drop, front drop.
Seat drop, knee drop.

**Fig. 9-12**

Seat drop, hands and knees drop.
Knee drop, back drop.
Hands and knees drop, back drop.
Seat drop, back drop.
Split jump, back drop.
Front drop, back drop.
Back drop, front drop.

## THREE STUNTS

Tuck jump, split jump, stag jump.
Tuck jump, half turn, split jump.
Stag jump, half turn, split jump.
Knee drop, seat drop, knee drop.
Seat drop, knee drop, hands and knees drop. See Fig. 9-13.
Hands and knees drop, seat drop, back drop.
Seat drop, knee drop, front drop.
Hands and knees drop, front drop, knee drop.
Seat drop, pass through a side split position in the air, land in a front drop.
Seat drop, half turn in the air landing in a seat drop (swivel hips).
Back drop, seat drop, front drop.
Back drop, hands and knees drop, back drop.
Front drop, half turn in the air landing in a front drop, facing the other end of
the tramp (turntable).
Back drop, pass through a hands and knees drop and roll sidewards while in
the air, landing in a back drop facing the other end (cradle).
Front drop, roll sidewards to a back drop, roll sidewards again in the air and
land in a front drop.

**Fig. 9-13**

The possibilities for further combinations are practically endless. They are limited only by the endurance of the performer. The ten bounce limit should be observed to prevent fatigue. Remember that a tired performer will have difficulty controlling his movements.

It should be noted that more difficult stunts, such as somersaults while in the air, have not been included here. They are for the more advanced performer and would not be within the capabilities of someone with coordination problems.

## ADDITIONAL TRAMPOLINE ACTIVITIES

Once students become fairly proficient in simple stunts there are several other possibilities for using the trampoline to improve coordination. The difficulty of the simpler stunts can be increased by having the student perform them with a blindfold on. This will remove reliance on visual focus and force the performer to pay more attention to kinesthesis.

Spotting for the blindfolded performer needs to be particularily accurate in terms of the directions given to the student so as to keep him in a safe position in the center of the tramp.

When a student has become fairly proficient in the rope jumping activities as well as on the trampoline these two can be combined. Many of the simpler rope jumping stunts can be done while bouncing on the trampoline. Again, the spotters should be especially vigilant in regard to the performer's position on the bed.

The chapter describing the use of small hand apparatus (Chapter 8) should also provide the reader with ideas for unusual trampoline stunts. Many of the activities using balls, for instance, would not only provide additional challenge, but also aid greatly in improving coordination by requiring the integration of many different physical factors in their accomplishment.

## FOR FURTHER REFERENCE

Cratty, B., *Trampoline Activities for Atypical Children*. Palo Alto, Peak, 1969.
Szypula, G., *Beginning Trampolining*. Belmont, California, Wadsworth, 1968.

# 10

## SPORTS ACTIVITY I:
## HOW TO THROW, CATCH AND KICK
## FOR COORDINATION

Though promoting coordinated activity has been the goal of the majority of activities in this text, coordination itself is not the end product for the student with coordination problems. Rather, the goal for him is successful participation in physical activities with other members of his peer group. Achieving coordinated movement is the first step in this direction. Applying this coordination to recognized sports activities is the second step and that is the concern of this and the following chapter.

The activities in these two chapters are designed for use by one person or sometimes two people working as partners. Their primary purpose is to combine the elements of coordinated activity which the student has been developing with the use of various pieces of sports equipment. The student needs to become not only familiar with the equipment itself but also with its appropriate use. The eventual goal is for participation in the activity with the entire class, but in the past the student with coordination problems has not been very successful at this. Now the learning must begin over again.

The activities included here are easy ones, suitable for beginners. Often the very simple drills are forgotten by the high school teacher who does not usually have lower level students. However, it is the easy activities that are needed by the student who is trying to improve his coordination, not only to build his skill but also to build his confidence in his own participation.

Since this is not a text on sports techniques, mention of such mechanics as grip, stance, body position, and general equipment handling is not included. This is not to imply that good form is not important, for good form, movement efficiency, and coordination all go together. However, the average teacher should already have a background in this area. Should anyone need further guidance in the subject of technique there are several suitable books included in the reference bibliography at the end of the chapter.

The activities in this chapter concern those sports involving throwing, catching and kicking. (Softball/Baseball is also included here though it could just as easily fit into Chapter 11.) The teacher may wish to have the students start with lightweight equipment made out of foam or plastic as opposed to the regulation items. Because it is easy to handle it would lessen both the chance and the fear of hurt fingers and toes while initial familiarity with the required movements is achieved. In addition, plastic equipment enables students to practice skills usually associated with outdoor participation, inside the gymnasium area.

Designed for use as warm-up activities or exercises to strengthen specific muscle groups, emphasis should first fall on familiarity with the equipment. Once this familiarity has been developed, controlled and skillful movement will follow and the uncoordinated student will soon be playing the game along with everyone else. For easy reference the activities have been arranged in order of difficulty.

## BASKETBALL

1. Jump into the air and reach up as high as possible. Practice jumping off two feet as well as one foot, and reaching with either or both arms.
2. Stand facing the wall. Chest pass the ball to the wall and catch it before it hits the ground. Make as many passes as possible in thirty seconds. Repeat with a variety of passes.
3. Stand in one place and bounce the ball around the body in a complete circle as fast as possible. Do not move the feet. Repeat in the opposite direction. Try it with the other hand.
4. Stand in one place in a straddle stand position. Bounce the ball in and out around the legs in a figure eight pattern. Repeat with the other hand. Do not move the feet.
5. Start dribbling and every time the teacher blows the whistle change the direction of travel.
6. Start dribbling and every time the teacher blows the whistle change hands.

7.  Assume a guarding stance and every time the teacher blows the whistle listen for a direction change. Move in the direction which the instructor indicated as if guarding an imaginary opponent.

8.  Set up a line of cones (or chairs or boxes), and dribble in a zig-zag pattern around the cones. Start with the cones several feet apart and gradually decrease the distance between them.

9.  Two persons pass the ball back and forth to each other. A variety of passes should be used and the receiver should not be told the type of pass ahead of time. Vary the distance apart as the type of pass is varied.

10. Dribble, and every time the instructor blows the whistle listen for a change of direction. The teacher should indicate direction changes such as forward, sideward, pivot, etc.

11. Stand a few feet away from the basket. Shoot for the basket and if missed try to get the rebound before it touches the floor. Try a variety of shots and vary the distance and angle from the basket. The student may dribble between shots.

12. Shoot from a stationary position in front of the basket. Get the rebound as quickly as possible and then shoot again from whatever spot the rebound is caught.

13. Face the wall. Jump off both feet as high as possible and while in the air release the ball in an overhead pass to the wall. Catch the ball and repeat.

14. Start at mid-court. Dribble toward the basket until just outside the lane. Without stopping the ball, check the dribble and shoot. Move immediately to get the rebound. Dribble back to mid-court and repeat.

15. Set up a line of cones, with the last cone about four feet from the wall. Zig-zag around the cones while dribbling. When the last cone is reached stop and pass the ball to the wall. Catch the return and dribble back to the start, zig-zagging back around the cones. Use a variety of passes during the activity.

16. Set up a line of cones going toward the basket. Zig-zag dribble around the cones. At the last one shoot. Get the rebound and zig-zag dribble back to the start. Set the line of cones at a variety of angles to the basket and try a variety of shots.

17. Two persons stand side-by-side about three feet apart at one end of the gym. One of them starts to run forward. The other passes the ball to the runner and then runs forward also. The receiver catches the ball, stops, and passes the ball back to the other person who is running past him. This sequence continues until they reach the other end of the room. A variety of passes should be used, each appropriate for the distance to be covered.

18. Two persons stand side-by-side about three feet apart at one end of the gym. One of them starts to run forward. The other passes the ball to the runner and then runs forward also. The receiver catches the ball, stops and passes the ball back to the other person who is running past him. This sequence continues until they reach the other end of the room.

When that happens the player with the ball attempts to shoot for a basket. The other player goes for the rebound and dribbles back to the starting line as quickly as possible.

19. One person starts with the ball at one end of the gym. The other starts half way between the two ends of the area. The object is for the person with the ball to dribble to the other end of the room. He may take any evasive action necessary, for the goal of the other person is to steal the ball and dribble it back to the starting line. Repeat with an exchange of places.

20. One person starts with the ball just outside the lane. He shoots for the basket and continues to shoot as long as he can get the rebound. He is not allowed to dribble. The other person tries to get the rebound. If and when he does, he shoots and the positions reverse. This may become more competitive between the two parties if goals made are scored.

21. HORSE—One player stands wherever he wants in front of the basket and shoots. If he makes it the other player must stand and shoot from exactly the same place. If the second player misses the identical shot he gets a letter of the word HORSE, such as H. If the first player misses his shot the second player may stand anywhere and the situation is reversed. The game is over when one player loses by getting all of the letters in the word HORSE.

22. Standing relatively close to the basket, shoot, and on the rebound jump and try for a tip-in. If missed get the rebound and try again.

## FOOTBALL

1. Toss the ball into the air and catch it before it hits the ground.
2. Two students pass the ball back and forth, each using a variety of passes without telling the other player what type of pass is coming.
3. Jog around the gym carrying the ball.
4. Jog carrying the ball and when the teacher blows the whistle change the ball to the other carrying arm.
5. Run the length of the area and when the teacher blows the whistle change direction by cutting on the diagonal.
6. Toss the ball high and away from the body. Run after it and catch it before it hits the ground.
7. Place a small target on the wall. Stand about two feet from the wall facing away from the target. Assume the crouched position of the center with the ball on the floor. Hike the ball backward to the target.
8. Two persons assume the positions of center and quarterback. The person as center practices hiking the ball back to his partner. Exchange positions and repeat.
9. Place the ball on a kicking tee. Stand on one foot and kick it as far as possible with the other foot.
10. From a standing position drop kick the ball as far as possible.

11. Place two vertical lines on the wall with the distance of the crossbar between them (or go outside and use the bar itself). Place the ball on the kicking tee fifteen yards away. From a standing position kick the ball at the target.

12. Perform exercise No. 11 using a running approach.

13. Place twelve tires in two parallel lines touching each other. Carrying the ball in the proper position run from one end of the tires to the other, stepping into the hole in each tire.

14. Run through the double line of tires and change the carrying arm of the ball at least once while running.

15. Two persons start at one end of the gym. One has the ball while the other runs out to receive a long pass. Exchange positions and repeat.

16. Suspend a hoop (or tire) from the ceiling (or crossbar). Use the hoop as a target through which the student must pass the ball. Vary the height of the target for different types of passes.

17. One student starts at one end of the gym carrying the ball. His objective is to run it to the other end, taking any evasive action necessary. Another person starts half way out on the floor and he tries to tag or grab the flag of the player doing the running. Exchange places and repeat.

## SOCCER

1. Place a twelve inch piece of tape along the bottom of a wall with its lower edge touching the floor. Kick the ball from a standing position using the tape as the target. Try kicking from a variety of angles and distances from the wall and alternate the foot used for kicking.

2. Kick the ball against the wall from a distance of about ten feet. As the ball comes back trap it. Gradually increase the force with which the ball is kicked.

3. Start dribbling the ball around the room and every time the teacher blows the whistle change direction.

4. Set up a line of cones (or chairs or boxes) and dribble in a zig-zag pattern around the cones. Start with the cones several feet apart and gradually shorten the distance between them.

5. Set up the line of cones so that it ends about ten feet from the tape target on the wall. Dribble in a zig-zag pattern around the cones. When the last cone is reached pass the ball to the tape. Trap the rebound and dribble around the cones back to the starting line.

6. Stand five feet from the wall. Kick the ball against the wall. As it rebounds kick it again. Do not back up and do not let the ball get past the five foot area. Perform as quickly as possible.

7. Set up two cones approximately ten feet apart. One person stands between and slightly in front of the cones to guard them. Set up a line of cones heading towards the guard. Dribble in a zig-zag pattern around the cones. When the last cone is reached kick the ball between the

cones, trying to get it past the person guarding them. If the attempt fails retrieve the ball, dribble back to the starting area and try again. Exchange positions and repeat.

8. Two persons pass the ball back and forth to each other. In receiving the ball a variety of means of trapping are used.

9. Place a tape line on the wall three feet off the ground. Stand five feet from the wall. Toss the ball against the wall above the tape line and as it rebounds use the body to knock the ball to the ground.

10. Two persons stand side-by-side about three feet apart at one end of the gym. One of them starts to run forward. The other passes the ball to the runner and then runs forward also. The receiver traps the ball and then passes it back to the other person who is running past him. This sequence continues until they reach the other end of the room.

11. Standing at one end of the area drop kick the ball as far as possible.

12. Two persons pass the ball back and forth between them without using their feet or legs. The ball must rebound off other parts of the body.

13. Two persons pass the ball back and forth between them without letting it touch the ground. Only legal soccer passes may be used.

14. One person starts with the ball at one end of the area. The other starts half way between the two ends of the room. He may take any evasive action necessary as he tries to dribble the ball to the other end of the room. The person in the middle should try to steal the ball from the one who is dribbling. If he does so, he should try to dribble it back to the starting line. Repeat with an exchange of places.

15. Toss the ball up into the air, and as it comes down bounce it off the head as in heading. Keep the ball in the air as long as possible using just the head.

16. Toss the ball into the air and as it comes down bounce it back into the air using one foot. When it comes down again bounce it back up off the other foot. Keep the ball bouncing back and forth between the feet.

## SOFTBALL

1. Toss the ball as high as possible into the air and catch it before it hits the ground.

2. Place the ball on a hitting tee. (One can be made by placing a cone on the seat of a chair and placing the ball on top of the cone.) Swing and hit the ball off the tee. Vary the body and/or arm position for a bunt, long hit, or field placement.

3. With tape, mark off a rectangular area on the wall corresponding to the strike zone of the batter—about one and a half feet off the floor, a foot wide, and about two and a half feet high. Use it as a target for practice pitching from the appropriate distance away.

4. Toss the ball away from the body and as high into the air as possible. Run up and catch it before it hits the ground.

5.  One person is the thrower and the other is the receiver. The two should be positioned at least thirty feet apart with the thrower remaining relatively stationary. He then throws to the receiver in a variety of ways, underhand high, grounder, overhead, overhand direct, etc. constantly changing the character of the throw. The receiver gets the ball as quickly as possible and throws it back. The two persons should exchange positions every twenty throws.

6.  With a partner, stand thirty feet apart with a tape line half way between. Roll the ball back and forth as fast as possible. The person catching it should attempt to do so before the ball crosses the half way line. He should then return to his original place to throw it back.

## FOR FURTHER REFERENCE

A complete list of sports activity texts can be found at the conclusion of Chapter 11.

# 11

## SPORTS ACTIVITY II:
## HOW TO HIT FOR COORDINATION

This, the second chapter on sports activities, contains those sports in which hitting, either with equipment or a part of the body, is the main form of participation. In many cases the student has to manipulate not one object but several. This complicates the problem somewhat and the coordination required is more intricate. Though softball does involve hitting, it was included in the previous chapter because it also involves throwing and catching. It should be kept in mind that these activities are designed for the beginner in the sport, both to familiarize him with the equipment and to strengthen him in the basic movements needed for participation.

*FIELD HOCKEY*

1. Stand ten feet from the wall. Hit the ball against the wall and as it comes back trap it. (*Note:* for indoor activity a rubber ball or puck may be used for practice purposes.)
2. Two persons pass the ball back and forth to each other. The ball should be stopped before the pass is returned and a variety of trapping methods should be used.
3. Dribble the ball around the area and every time the teacher blows the whistle change direction.
4. Straddle stand, holding the stick in the two-handed carrying position. Lunge to the right and extend the stick in the same direction. Return to the starting position and repeat lunging to the left. When reaching,

stretch as far as possible such as when stealing the ball from another player.

5. Jog around the area carrying the stick in the two-handed carrying position. Every five steps stop and lunge forward, extending the stick forward as far as possible with just the stick arm.

6. Jog around the area carrying the stick. Every time the teacher blows the whistle change direction and lunge at the same time.

7. Stand ten feet from a corner. Hit the ball against the wall on the left. As the ball comes back hit it immediately toward the wall on the right. Continue hitting it against the two walls on an alternating basis.

8. Set up a line of cones leaving three feet between each cone. Dribble in a zig-zag pattern in and out between the cones. As skill increases decrease the distance between the cones.

9. Two persons stand in the bully position. They perform the bully, each attempting to gain control of the ball and dribble to his own goal line. After the bully the person who does not get the ball can try to steal it during the dribble.

10. Set a series of cones at varying distances from a hitting line and parallel to it. From a stationary position hit the ball to one of the cones. Retrieve the ball and dribble back to the hitting line. Move to the next cone and repeat. The ball should go to the cone chosen, that is the target.

11. Two persons stand side-by-side about three feet apart at one end of the area. One of them starts to run forward. The other passes the ball to the runner and then runs forward also. The receiver stops the ball and then directs it back to the other person who is running past him. This sequence continues until they reach the other end of the area.

12. One person starts with the ball at one end of the field. The other starts half way between the two ends of the area. The object is for the person with the ball to dribble to the other end, taking any evasive action necessary. The other person should try to take the ball away and dribble it back to the starting area. Repeat with an exchange of places.

13. One person stands in front of two cones spread five feet apart. The other person attempts to hit the ball past the guard and between the cones from a distance of at least five feet away.

14. One person stands in front of two cones spread five feet apart. The other person starts at least half way to the other end of the area, and a line of cones is placed between him and the goal area. He then dribbles in and out around the cones. When he reaches the last one he attempts to hit the ball past the guard and between the cones. The guard attempts to send the ball out of the area.

## GOLF

1. Grip the club with only one hand and place it with the heel of the club on the ground. Keeping the arm still, rotate the wrist and lift the club head

off the ground and directly up until it is perpendicular to the body and parallel to the ground. Lower the club and repeat with the other hand.

2.  Grasp the club with one hand and place the heel of the club on the ground. Keeping the arm and wrist straight lift the club sideward as far as possible and then allow it to swing down and through to the other side as far as possible. Continue the pendulum swing. Repeat with the other arm.

3.  Grasp the club with one hand and place the heel of the club on the ground. Keeping the arm straight and in place flex the wrist, lifting the club off the ground and to the side. Then move the wrist through extension into hyperextension swinging the club back past the ground and up to the other side. Continue the pendulum swing, keeping the arm still. Repeat with the other hand.

4.  Perform numbers 1, 2, and 3 with both hands gripping the club.

5.  Place several tape markings on the wall at a variety of heights. Standing at least fifteen feet away try to hit the ball against one of the pieces of tape. Choose the target tape ahead of time and then select the club and type of swing according to how high the ball has to go to hit the tape.

6.  Place a paper cup on its side in the middle of a piece of carpet with short nap or on well cut grass. Use this for putting practice from a variety of distances.

## TENNIS

1.  Bounce the ball on the floor with the racket hand, keeping the wrist straight and the palm and the fingers flat.

2.  Bounce the ball into the air off the flat palm of the racket hand. Keep the wrist flat. Continue the bouncing as long as possible.

3.  Bounce the ball on the ground and as it comes back up, hit it toward the wall using the flat palm of the racket hand. Keep the wrist and elbow straight. Let the ball bounce on the floor after it hits the wall and hit it again.

4.  Bounce the ball on the floor and then hit it against the wall using the flat palm of the racket hand. Continue to volley it against the wall without letting it touch the ground. Try to keep the wrist and elbow straight.

5.  Alternately bounce the ball down to the floor and then up into the air with the flat palm of the racket hand.

6.  With the hand opposite to the racket hand toss the ball into the air and catch it again. Try to make the toss as straight as possible.

7.  Toss the ball into the air with one hand and reaching high overhead hit it with the flat palm of the other hand.

8.  Repeat numbers 1, 2, 3, 4, 5, and 7 using the tennis racket.

9.  One person stands on the base line and the other stands on the same side of the net but close to it. The player near the net bounces the ball to the other player who volleys it over the net with the forehand drive. Repeat with the backhand drive.

10. Place a tape line on the wall at the same height as the top of the tennis net. Use this line for serving and volleying practice.

## VOLLEYBALL

1. Jump and reach as high into the air as possible. Practice taking off from either one or both legs, and reaching up with either or both hands.
2. Toss the ball into the air at least two feet above the head. Use the opposite hand of the one used to write with. Try for a straight toss and catch the ball with the same hand.
3. Toss the ball against the wall at a point at least seven feet off the floor. Then volley the ball against the wall as many times as possible at this height.
4. Place the hands and forearms in the dig position. Repeatedly bounce the ball into the air with the hands in this position as in digging.
5. Toss the ball into the air and continue to volley it straight up with the setting action of the hands and arms. Keep it up as long as possible.
6. Toss the ball into the air and keep it in the air by alternately hitting it with a set and a dig.
7. Two persons volley the ball back and forth over the net.
8. Two persons set the ball back and forth to each other on the same side of the net.
9. One person stands a few feet away from the other and tosses him the ball, aiming between the knees and hips. The person receiving the ball digs it as high as possible.
10. Toss the ball into the net and as it comes out of the net dig it high up into the air.
11. One person stands on one side of the net and tosses the ball so that it just clears the net as it goes over. The other student stands on the other side of the net and attempts to block the tossed ball.
12. Standing on the same side of the net, and at arm's distance from it one person tosses the ball straight into the air as high as possible. The other person then attempts to spike it over the net.
13. Standing on the same side of the net and at arm's distance from it one person tosses the ball straight into the air as high as possible. The other person then attempts to tip or lightly tap it over.

## FOR FURTHER REFERENCE

American Association for Health, Physical Education and Recreation, *Tennis Group Instruction*. Washington D.C., AAHPER, 1963.

Armbruster, Irwin, and Musker, *Basic Skills in Sports for Men and Women*, St. Louis, Mosby, 1967.

Dewitt, R. T., and K., Dugan, *Teaching Individual and Team Sports*. Englewood Cliffs, New Jersey, Prentice-Hall, Inc., 1972.

Division for Girls and Women's Sports. Sports Guide Series. AAHPER, Washington D.C.

Hartman, P. E., *Volleyball Fundamentals*. Columbus, Merrill, 1972.

Laver, R. *How to Play Championship Tennis*. New York, Macmillian, 1965.

Meyer, M. H., and M. M. Schwartz, *Team Sports for Girls and Women*. Philadelphia, Saunders, 1965.

National Golf Foundation, *Nine Comprehensive Golf Lessons*. Chicago, National Golf Foundation, 1963.

Prentice-Hall Sports Series. Englewood Cliffs, Prentice-Hall, Inc.

Sports Illustrated Library, New York, Lippincott.

Waters, E. C., P. E. Haek, and J. V. Squires, *Soccer*. Menasha, Wisconsin, Banter, 1967.

West, J., *Basketball My Way*. Englewood Cliffs, New Jersey, Prentice-Hall, Inc., 1973.

# 12

# RELAXATION: A MUST FOR COORDINATION

Uncertainty, doubt, fear of failure, and dislike of activity combined with awkward, inefficient movements all tend to build up tension in the uncoordinated student. This tension, both physical and mental, in turn increases the uncertainty and awkwardness of the person involved. The resulting tension cycle needs to be broken in order for an improvement in coordination to take place. The tension needs to be replaced by relaxation. This chapter will concern itself with the physical aspects of obtaining this relaxation.

Once the student is able to control the amount of physical tension in his body and put a limit on the amount of tension which he allows to build up, he will find movement easier. A lower level of tension will free his muscles for other things. Flexibility will increase and strength will improve. As this begins to happen his motor skills will also improve and though no direct action has been taken on his mental state, that too will improve. The tension cycle will begin to work in reverse as successful physical activity builds mental confidence and pleasure in accomplishment. It is this relaxation which will allow the student to develop to his full potential of coordination.

## SHORT BREAKS TO RELAX DURING ACTIVITY

Tension is something that has a cumulative effect on the human body. Though very little tension may be present at the start of an activity, it can build up quickly. The activities in this section are designed to provide a break in whatever is taking place in class. They are short in duration, each lasting from only a few seconds to one or two minutes. It is not necessary to prolong them unless an extreme amount of tension or fatigue is present. In such cases any of the activities could be continued for a longer period of time as a cool down exercise. Usually, instead of prolonging a break activity, repeating it frequently during class brings better results. This will not only vary the routine of the class but also keep the tension at a minimum level during a majority of the time.

*DEEP BREATHS*—In either a comfortable sitting or standing position take a deep breath, inflating the lungs to their maximum size. Then exhale, emptying the lungs of as much air as possible. Both the inhale and the exhale should be done slowly. Do not exceed four repetitions.

*GENTLE SHAKING*—In a comfortable standing or sitting position gently shake the arms and the legs. For best results do them one at a time.

*HANG*—From a straddle standing position, bend forward from the waist and just let the upper body hang toward the floor, arms dangling from the shoulders. After a few seconds return slowly to a standing position by slowly uncurling the spine, bringing the head up last.

*WALK-A-LAP*—At a comfortable pace, walk a lap of the gym. Take a moderate size stride and let the arms swing freely from the shoulders.

## RELAXATION EXERCISES

In order for conscious relaxation to take place a person first needs to be able to distinguish a relaxed state from a tense one. Though in many cases the teacher can control the tension level in the students by using the short break activities described earlier, if the student is to become able to regulate the level of tension within his own body, he needs to learn to feel the difference between a relaxed and a tense or contracted state. The exercises in this section will help him do this. They consist of combinations of extreme tension and complete relaxation in movement so that the performer can learn to feel the great difference between the two. Because they involve a state of almost complete relaxation they could also be used as short break activities or as cooling down exercises at the completion of the other strenuous activity. To aid the student in his concentration on what he is feeling it is suggested that the exercises be performed with the eyes closed. If a student becomes dizzy during exercises requiring breath control, have him stop the exercise and caution him not to do as many repetitions next time.

The reader may notice the similarity between the description of the complete tension versus complete relaxation aspect of these exercises and that of the contraction aspect of isometric exercises. There are many isometric exercises which can also help the student to realize and feel the difference in contraction of the various muscle groups. Many such exercises can be found in Chapter 2 of this text.

COLLAPSE AND STAND—In a straddle standing position bend from the waist and let the top half of the body fall forward into the hang position. Then slowly realign the trunk by raising and straightening one vertebra at a time until the head is lifted to its original position. See Fig. 12-1.

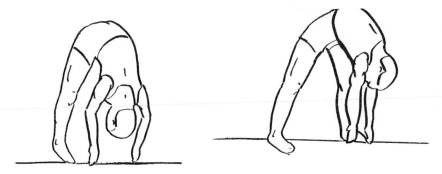

**Fig. 12-1**

CONTROLLED BREATHING—Sitting position with the knees bent and the bottoms of the feet flat against each other. Let the hands rest on the ankles. Let the upper body collapse, dropping the head and chest close to the feet. At the same time exhale as much air as possible from the lungs. Then slowly resume the original sitting position by uncurling the spine one vertebra at a time. As the body uncurls, slowly inhale until the lungs are full.

INHALE AND CONTRACT—Straddle stand. Take a deep breath and at the same time contract the abdominal muscles as much as possible. Hold for ten seconds. Exhale and relax the abdomen. Repeat twice. See Fig. 12-2.

STRETCH AND TUCK—From a comfortable back lying position roll sideward onto the left side. Pull the knees to the chest, tuck the head and wrap the arms as tightly as possible around the legs. At the same time inhale and hold the breath and the tight grasp of the legs for five seconds. Release the hold of the legs, exhale and roll back onto the back, letting the body go limp. Repeat rolling to the other side. See Fig. 12-3.

TOTAL CONTRACTIONS—In a back lying position with the eyes closed make a fist with the right hand and clinch that fist as tight as possible. Hold for five seconds and then release the fist. Then using the same arm make a fist only half as tight, hold, and release. Make another one again reducing the contrac-

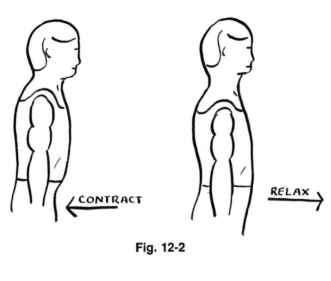

**Fig. 12-2**

**Fig. 12-3**

tion by half. Then just think a fist but do not actually make one. Repeat the whole sequence with the other arm. With the legs, point one foot as much as possible and follow the same tension reduction sequence. Repeat with the other leg. Contract the body's abdominal muscles and follow the tension reduction sequence again. Complete the exercise by contracting the neck muscles and bringing the chin to the chest and again follow the established pattern of repeating the contractions at half strength.

# 13

# USING MUSIC AS AN AID
# TO COORDINATION

In almost any physical activity we do we are constantly being bombarded by sound. Voices, equipment sounds, building noise all send stimuli through our auditory reception system to our brain and we usually respond in some way to the effect it has on us. Music is one form of this auditory input and it can be used in a variety of ways to improve coordination. First, it can be used as a background for whatever activity is taking place; second, it can be used as a direct aid to developing rhythmic movement; and last, but not least, it can be used to help the uncoordinated student gain more control over his consciously directed movements.

The most popular and probably the easiest form of music for the physical education teacher to use is phonograph records. They are readily available and most schools have phonographs as standard equipment. It does not take an elaborate stereo system to use records successfully. However, the machine used should have a good needle and the records should be free from scratches. It will be easier to maintain the equipment in good condition if the needle is set down and lifted carefully and if the records are held by the edges, avoiding placing the fingers on the groves.

If the school does not have a record collection or the funds to begin one there are several other ways to provide the desired music. In most large cities the public library has a record collection available for loan as do many large universities. If a tape recorder is available it is easy to make tapes from the radio or television or even from live concerts in the area. Local radio stations, especially FM broadcasters, publish program guides ahead of time. If desirable programs fall during the school day they can be tuned in directly in class.

Included in the various sections of this chapter are suggested recordings. They are meant to serve as examples of the type of music for the purpose being discussed. Where a selection is only available on one particular label the name of the company and the record number has been included. If the selection is available on several record labels just the name of the composer is given. Though most local record stores could order desired records if they were not in stock, a list of record companies and their addresses is included at the end of the chapter.

Though initially the teacher will want to select carefully the music used, as the students become more familiar with the place of music in the class they should be encouraged to bring in their own favorite records or tapes for the rest of the class to use.

## MUSIC AS A BACKGROUND

Though the focus of the student's attention may be on teacher-directed or self-directed activity, having appropriate music playing in the background may bring about a surprising improvement in performance. Not only does it enhance relaxation but it also stimulates movement and sets the mood for the activity. It does not have to be loud for it is just a "background" for concentration on other things. The effect it has is a subconscious one rather than one based on attention. In fact, it is not even necessary for the teacher to call attention to having the music on. Just let it be there and watch the results.

*Music for Relaxation*—One of the big problems of the uncoordinated student is being able to relax while engaged in physical activity. As was mentioned in Chapter 12 the two main causes for this are physical restrictions and psychological inhibitions. Muscles that are not used will atrophy. They will lose their ability to lengthen and as a result the motion of the joint involved will be restricted. This in turn hampers the motor activity of the individual. The uncoordinated student is not usually fond of physical activity and as a result his muscles do not get an adequate amount of stretching activity. Music itself will not improve the elasticity of these muscles. However, the effect of music on the mental attitude of the performer will.

When a person cannot move well and feels uncomfortable he is not usually at ease when asked to move around the gym. His muscles feel tight and after several days of exercise they may also feel sore. He may fear being injured if he does any strenuous activity. His concentration on his physical problems may greatly inhibit his performance. He is anything but relaxed. Music can play a big part in changing this situation.

Because of the close link between the senses and the emotions, music, through the sense of hearing, has long been known to affect the emotions. Mothers put on soothing music to put babies to sleep. Busy offices play background music to provide an environment more conducive to work. Dentists use music to take the mind of the patient off the drill. For some undescribable reason music directly affects the psychological set of the listener. Appropriate music playing in the background of the physical education class will not only give the performer something to concentrate on besides himself but also it will relax his mind, make him feel more at ease, lessen the tension and reduce inhibiting mental activity. This in turn will relax his total nervous system and its rigid hold over muscular activity. Once this has happened he will be much freer to move, and as a result his whole body will be much more relaxed. Movement will improve because the body will now be free to move.

The type of music most conducive to relaxation is that of a slower, quieter quality. Melodies of a smooth, flowing nature carried by instrumentalists rather than vocalists work best. In addition, some very good results have been achieved with recordings of natural environments such as the ocean or forest. Some examples of background music to aid relaxation include:

*Andre Kostelanetz' Greatest Hits of the 60'S*—Columbia LPN 0868.
*Background Moods*—Readers Digest.
*Environments I and II*—Syntonic 1/10 XEP.
*Pops Goes West*—RCA LSC 3008.
*Primitiva: The Exotic Sounds of Martin Denny*—Liberty LRP 3087.
*Relaxation–Impulse Control Through Relaxation*—Educational Activities AR 655.
*Swan Lake* by Tchaikovsky.
*Traumerei* by Schumann.

Many of the selections listed in the section on mood would also be appropriate here.

*Music for Stimulation*—With the large quantity of music being heard every day practically everyone at some time or other has heard music that has made him want to get up and move around. What better place to want to move around than the physical education class? As was mentioned before, motivation is a definite problem for the uncoordinated student. But the right kind of music can make him feel like he wants to do something rather than sit still.

Having music on as the students come into class helps set the atmosphere for the entire class period. Even if the record is turned off after class starts or a change is made to a different type of music the active mood which has been set will tend to prevail. In addition, having music on at the start of class will probably be a change from the way in which previous classes have started and as such it is likely to provide for an initial pleasurable contact with the class situation.

Lively music, something with rhythm or a beat, seems to bring the greatest response. Swing, jazz, rock, or just march music played by a good band would do. However, here is an opportunity for the interests of the students to help involve them in class. Whatever music is currently popular would be the best choice. Any local record store or radio station should provide a source of materials until the students start bringing their own records and though not all of the currently popular things would be suitable there should be an adaquate number to choose from.

In addition to current popular music some other examples of music to stimulate activity are:

*African Concert*—Phillips PCC 214.
*Ages of Rock*—MGM E/SE 4502.
*Fiddle Faddle*—RCA LSC 2638.
*Firewords*—Columbia ML 6024.
*Leroy Anderson Conducts Leroy Anderson*—Decca DL 78865.
*Magic Fire Music*—Columbia ML 6101.
*Switched on Bach*—Columbia MS 7194.

*Music to Establish a Mood*—Often times the benefit that a student gets from an exercise or activity is dependent upon the attitude with which he approaches that activity—not necessarily his willingness to participate or his attention to the correct mechanics of performance, but rather his feeling or empathy for the character of the action. It is a distinction of quality rather than quantity. Some moves are meant to be strong and forceful, while some are meant to be weak or gentle. Some may be lively, and others quite heavy and ponderous.

In order to achieve this expression of feeling in movement the student must be able to understand that there is such a feeling. Though it is possible to see the difference if the movement is demonstrated, it is necessary for the student to feel the expressed quality himself before he can perform it. Here is where the right kind of music can be an asset.

Here the selection of music is dependent entirely upon the mood of the activity it is to accompany. Pieces will tend to be shorter, since what might be good for one exercise might be unsuitable for another. Though the instructor could change records as the mood changed, it would probably be more convenient if a tape recording were used. It could be prepared ahead of time, containing only the selections that would be used in class, and it could be taped in the order in which they would be needed. Some examples of music to establish a mood include:

*Also Sprach Zarathustra* by Strauss.
*Death Valley Suite* by Grofé.
*Firebird Suit* by Stravinsky.
*In a Wild Sanctuary*—Warner Brothers 1850.
*Isle of the Dead* by Rachmaninoff.
*Nature's Music Recorded Live on this Planet*—Yorkshire 27015.
*Nite on Bald Mountain* by Moussorgsky.
*Our Man in Hollywood Henry Mancini*—RCA LPN 2604.
*Ride of the Valkyrides* by Wagner.

## DEVELOPING RHYTHMIC MOVEMENT

In addition to providing a background to physical activity music can play a valuable role in developing that movement. Practically every physical action that is made has rhythm. Some of them are obvious—walking, writing a letter, eating dinner, brushing the teeth. However, many of the rhythms are not noticed because they are not sustained over a long enough period of time. But the beat is there.

It is the presence of this beat that directly aids the development of rhythmic movement for it gives the participant something to focus on, a point of orientation. Using this point of orientation, he can improve not only his stationary and locomotor movements but his manipulative ones as well, for it will help him to control the timing of his activities. Once the timing has been controlled and a rhythm established in simple movements he will be able to exert more control over the more complicated sports activities.

*Rhythm and Stationary Movement*—Just as the easiest exercises to learn were those which were performed with the body remaining on relatively one spot, the easiest way to introduce the aspect of rhythm to movement is with movements which allow the body to remain in one place as opposed to those in which the person moves around the room.

The counts of the exercise should correspond to the beats of the music. Thus, the first thing the student needs to do is learn the counts and corresponding actions of the exercise. The next step is learning to feel the beat of the music. It is not necessary that he be able to count it measure by measure but it would help.

The two beat structures that are the most useful in establishing rhythmic movement are those based on two counts and those based on three counts. In either case the first beat of the measure usually gets the accent or heaviest pulse. Then by counting it and the number of beats that follow it before the next heavy beat comes the listener can determine if the rhythm is based on two or three.

If the listener counts two, four, or eight beats, the rhythm is based on two. March music is an excellent example of this. Exercises which have two, four, or eight counts would fit this music beat. If the listener counts three or six beats the rhythm is based on three. An excellent example of this type is the waltz, to which exercises which involve a swinging motion fit best.

The teacher should listen to and count the music first, before class, to determine the beat. Then in class the students should also listen first, to determine the beat. They can also be asked to tap or clap along with the music to help them get the feel of it. They can clap louder on the accent beat or clap that beat and tap the others to distinguish it from the others. Once the student has the beat he can then add the performance of his exercise.

For the teacher who does not have a good reference collection of music or does not have the time to listen to and evaluate the music before it is used there are many records on the market which have already done this for the listener. Exercises have been set to music complete with verbal instructions right on the record. It is helpful if the teacher orders such records on a trial basis for there is a wide variety in the offerings available, not only in the activity content, but also in the manner of presentation. Some have just the exercise explanation with music, while others have this and then several repetitions at increasingly faster speeds, concluding with just the music without any verbal cues. These records come with all kinds of music and exercise combinations and a little bit of looking and listening should provide the teacher with what he needs. Musical selections which would aid stationary rhythmic movement include:

*And the Beatles Go on for Physical Education*—Educational Activities KEA 8080.

*And the Beat Goes on for Physical Education*—Educational Activities KEA 5010.
*Chicken Fat*—Capitol CF 1000.
*Cooperative Activities*—Educational Activities KEA 9005.
*Country and Western Music for Rhythmic Exercises*—Educational Activities KEA 5030.
*Danish Balance Exercises*—Educational Activities AR 45.
*Graded Physical Fitness Exercises for Boys*—Educational Activities K 3020.
*Swedish Conditioning and Exercise Program*—Educational Activities 10-SWE.

*Music for Locomotion*—Moving the entire body through space is a much more difficult task then remaining in one place and moving just one body part. But here too, this task can be made much easier by giving the student a reference point for his movement. The type of music chosen depends on the type of locomotor activity. Movement based on two or four counts such as the walk would require music based on two or four counts, such as a march; while a skip, essentially a three beat movement, would need music based on three beats, such as a waltz.

In choosing music for locomotor activities the teacher should be aware that the selections need to be longer to accomodate the duration of time it takes to move across the floor. Because it is more difficult to find suitable selections recorded at various speeds it would be highly desirable to use a phonograph that has a variable speed adjustment. Examples of music suitable for locomotor activity would include:

*Basic Dance Tempos*—Educational Activities HYP 501A.
*Basic Popular Music*—Educational Activities AR 509.
*In London with the Coldstream Guards*—RCA LPM 1674.
*Jumpnastics*—Educational Activities KEA 6000.
*Floor Exercise Music*—Educational Activities K 8010.

*Music for Manipulation*—The uncoordinated student usually has a great deal of difficulty controling the equipment he must use to participate in sports activities successfully. Previous chapters (Chapters 7, 8, 10, and 11) provide many activities to help him overcome this problem. However, most of these activities could be enhanced by the addition of music. Just as music provided a focus for body movement, so can it establish a frame of reference for manipulative activities.

The easiest way to use music for this purpose is to first find music with a clear beat, one that can be easily picked up from the music. Then ask the student to perform whatever he is doing—bouncing a ball, rolling a hoop, dribbling a puck or jumping rope—in time to the music. It might mean one bounce or whatever, to each beat, or it might mean several. This would depend upon the speed of the record as well as the activity involved. However, the student should be able to establish and maintain his activity in time with the music. Selections of music to accompany manipulation activities might include:

*Danish Ball Rhythms*—Educational Activities AR 44.
*Musical Ball Skills*—Educational Activities AR 30.
*Rhythmic Ball Gymnastics*—Educational Activities EA K 4030.
*Rhythmic Gymnastics Using Hand Apparatus*—Educational Activities K 5040.
*Rhythmic Parachute Play*—Educational Activities KEA 6020.
*Rhythmic Rope Jumping*—Educational Activities K 4000.
*Rope Skipping*—Educational Activities HYP 12.
*Rope Skipping–Rhythms, Rhymes and Routines*—Educational Activities AR 536.

## MOVEMENT CONTROL THROUGH IMPROVISATION

Improvisation implies a making up as one goes along. Nothing is planned ahead of time and no two improvisations ever turn out the same. It is highly related to feeling and emotion for the participant does whatever he feels appropriate for the situation. There is no right or correct way to respond in an improvisation situation, for everyone's feelings are different.

But if there is no right or wrong how does the uncoordinated student improve his control over his movement? Improvisation is not a random or chance activity. It is an expressive one and as such a great deal of control is needed if the participant is going to be able to adaquately express what he feels. He will have to first identify this feeling and then select and perform the movements which he feels will express this feeling. It is this striving for expressive quality that will help him gain greater control over his bodily movement.

*Breaking away from Stereotypes*—Improvisation is an extremely difficult activity even for the average student. For the student with coordination problems it will probably seem impossible, not because the mechanics of the movement are difficult, but because of the psychological problems involved. Here the student is not only allowed but requested to "do his own thing." However, in the past his own thing usually wasn't very good and he knew it. As a result he won't be very eager to try it again.

It is up to the teacher to help him overcome this inhibition by being sure he understands the purpose of the activity, emphasizing helping him to gain control over his own body. In addition, the initial class periods for this activity should be structured in such a way that the participant will not feel threatened by it. This can be done quite easily by blindfolding the class. They will not be able to see anyone else, and more important, no one will be able to see them. This also means that they should refrain from locomotor activities, remaining in one place rather than moving around.

For each musical selection used a problem should be set for the student. At the start these should be fairly concrete statements, providing a structure for the student to experiment within. For example, if the Saint-Saens "Carnival of the Animals" was the musical selection used the student might be asked to become whatever animal he thinks he hears. He may or may not be the same one that is being played. It does not really matter. What does matter is the way in which he expresses or portrays the animal. He should be encouraged to try a variety of movements involving different combinations of body parts. He should avoid repetition of similar movements. This is difficult for the uncoordinated student since he usually has a limited number of familar actions to choose from and will need to be encouraged to experiment.

Once the student has become involved in his own innovative productivity the blindfolds can be removed. Then a constructive part of each class can be spent viewing and commenting on the movement of others. The self-confidence of the student will only begin to increase when he begins to receive peer acceptance. Emphasis during the class discussions should be on improvement shown and on ways of bettering performance.

*Improving Expression*—As the student develops the ability to transform concrete ideas into movement, he should also begin to work with the physical expression of abstractions. The music chosen should have definite emotional qualities and the student should be asked to reflect these qualities in his movement. Feelings of strength or power, sharpness or harshness, gentleness, pain, joy, merriment, despair are just a few of the many possibilities. Again, variety in the movements used is important. Students should try for total body involvement, responding to the feelings that they receive from the music.

*Abstract Creativity*—Some pieces of music have neither a concrete theme nor strong emotional content but they still provide an interesting stimulus for movement. The student is then free to experiment in any way he wants—with creating different shapes, moving through various levels, working with contrasting speeds, moving in response to a partner, or just exploring space. It is doing what the music tells them to do in whatever way they want to do it.

Improvisation, though difficult, can be a highly rewarding experience for the student. As a final test of his ability to adapt and create ask him to respond to a variety of musical pieces in a short space of time. If a tape recorder is available record bits of music (fifteen to thirty seconds each) sequentially on the tape. Try to avoid having two similar types of music in a row. Then just play the tape. The variety of musical selections should be equaled by the variety of movements. A student able to handle this situation has gained a great deal of control over his physical capabilities.

Appropriate music for improvisation might include:

*Carnival of the Animals* by Saint-Saens.
*Chilling, Thrilling Sounds of the Haunted House*—Disney DQ 1257.
*Fantasy in Orbit*—Phillips PHS 600-189.
*Grand Canyon Suite* by Grofe'.
*In Sound from Way Out*—Vanguard VSD 79222.
*Kaleidoscopic Variations*—Vanguard VSD 79284.
*Missa Luba*—Phillips PCC 206.
*Nutcracker Suite* by Tchaikovsky.
*Pictures at an Exhibition* by Moussorgsky.
*Pines of Rome* by Respighi.
*Planets* by Holst.
*Rodeo* by Copland.
*Sorcerer's Apprentice* by Dukas.

## LIST OF RECORD COMPANIES

Bowmar Records, 4921 Santa Monica Blvd., Los Angeles, California, 90021.
Children's Record Guild, Greystone Corporation, 100 Sixth Avenue, New York, New York 10013.
Columbia Records, 51 West 52nd Street, New York, New York, 10019.
Decca Records, 50 West 57th Street, New York, New York, 10019.
Educational Activities, Box 392, Freeport, New York, 11520.
Enrichment Records, 246 Fifth Avenue, New York, New York, 10001.
Folkways Records, 117 West 46th Street, New York, New York, 10036.
Kimbo Records, 1019 16th Avenue, S., Nashville, Tennessee, 37212.
Kjos Music Company, 525 Busse Highway, Parkwidge, Illinois, 60068.
RCA Records Division, 155 East 24th Street, New York, New York, 10010.

## FOR FURTHER REFERENCE

Andrews, G., *Creative Rhythmic Movement for Children*. Englewood Cliffs, New Jersey, Prentice-Hall, Inc., 1954.

Carlquist, M., and T. Amylong, *Balance and Rhythm in Exercise*. New York, Viking, 1951.

Gaston, E. T., *Music in Therapy*. New York, Macmillan, 1968.

Gates, A. A., *Movement–A Dancer's View*. Minneapolis, Burgess, 1968.

# 14

# PLANNING THE TOTAL PROGRAM:
# HOW TO DO IT

Realizing that there are many students in physical education classes that have coordination problems and need help is the first step toward building a sound program. But there is a large gap between realizing this need and using the activities in this text to meet it. This gap should be filled with careful planning and preparation in the selection of activities. Helping the teacher in establishing guidelines for putting together a total physical education program for the student with coordination problems is the object of this chapter.

## HOW TO BEGIN

As stated above, recognizing the need is the first step. The second is doing something about this need by identification of the students who appear to have coordination problems. How to do this is considered in more detail in Chapter 1. However, just as a reminder, let us state that a teacher's observation of a student's performance on a day-to-day basis is probably one of the easiest and most appropriate means of evaluation.

Once the students have been selected the teacher needs to decide whether these students should remain in their regular class or be placed in a special class whose entire population is made up of students with similar problems. Because of the great variety in school situations it is impossible to say definitely which would be best. However, the following factors should be considered by anyone having to make this decision:

1.  What kind of placement would the student prefer? Some students would prefer the privacy of a small, special class while others would be embarrassed by being removed from their regular class. How the student feels about the class he will be in should be a primary consideration.
2.  How many students in a particular class have been identified as needing help? If a large percentage of a group was having difficulties the whole group would probably benefit from this program.
3.  How flexible is the school schedule? Students in very large or crowded schools may not be able to schedule into special classes. They may, however, be willing to come before or after school for special help and do much of their work independently if they have help getting started.
4.  How many students are there in the class? The smaller the group the more time there is for individual help.
5.  How much equipment is available for class use? Classes should be kept small enough so that each participant can have his own equipment, with sharing kept to a minimum.
6.  How large is the room? The smaller the floor space the smaller the size of the group should be to give each student maximum space to move around in.

Once the groups of students are set the actual work of the program can begin.

## INDIVIDUALIZING INSTRUCTION

No two students will be identical in the movement problems they have or the way they feel about physical activity. The needs of the class will be as varied and numerous as there are students in it. Therefore, in order for each one of these students to develop to his maximum potential the teacher has to individualize instruction as much as possible. This procedure begins with goal setting. The teacher should attempt to meet with each student separately to discuss:

1.  Areas of strength or good performance in physical activity.
2.  Areas of weakness in physical activity.

3. Possibilities for improvement of weaknesses.
4. Areas in which new interest may be developed.

The teacher needs to consider how the student assesses his own performance and needs for improvement in addition to whatever professional evaluation has been made, since goal setting, to be successful, has to be a joint effort.

After meeting with the individual students the teacher then has the job of planning activities to help each one reach his own goals. This text provides a great variety of resource material to choose from and it has been arranged progressively from the most fundamental to the very complex, including:

1. Exercises to develop the individual areas of strength and flexibility and to improve the general fitness level of the individual. Exercises can be selected to emphasize a particular part of the body, if desired. Though most students will need some form of basic exercise, the particular ones chosen should reflect individual areas of weakness. (Chapters 2 and 3.)
2. Activities combining various exercise forms into more purposeful, skilled manipulation of the body, requiring the development of balance as well as fluidity of motion. (Chapters 4 and 5.)
3. Activities to improve endurance by increasing the speed of the activity or prolonging it over a more extended period of time. (Chapter 6.)
4. Activities involving the use of additional equipment to help the student to develop his coordination in relation to another object while continuing to improve his balance, flexibility, strength and endurance. (Chapters 7 and 8.)
5. Activities involving performance in a different medium using the trampoline. (Chapter 9.)
6. Activities designed to help the student apply his developing coordination to sports activities in which he is interested. (Chapters 10 and 11.)
7. Activities adding the stimulation and structure of music to movement. (Chapter 13.)
8. Activities to help the student develop relaxation in movement. (Chapter 12.)

Choosing a variety of activities will not only increase the interest of the students but also help them to develop in all of the fundamental areas of functioning that constitute coordinated movement.

Some students may experience difficulty with an activity. If the teacher notices this and is unable to improve performance with simple verbal correction or demonstration it may be helpful to consider the following:

1. Is the student ready for this particular activity or should he be doing something more fundamental in the progession and work up to it?
2. Is the student physically, perceptually and/or mentally capable of activity in this area or does he need to develop more fundamental capabilities first?
3. Does the student have the potential for development in this area or does a physical, perceptual, and/or mental impairment preclude this development from taking place?
4. Does the student have a physical, perceptual and/or mental impairment which requires an adaptation of the activity?

Students having deficits in the areas such as muscle strength or flexibility will be fairly easy to detect, and improvement will come through repetitive performance. However, students with permanent physical disabilities or problems of perception may have to concentrate on improving their performance through adaptation and compensation, for by the time these students are of high school age the possibilities for remediation are quite small. Whatever the situation, each student should be encouraged to develop his own skills to the maximum with the end result or goal being enjoyment of successful participation in some physical activity with his peer group.

## EVALUATION

No successful program would be complete without some means of determining the amount of progress being made by those participating in it. A person does not become coordinated overnight. It is a long and arduous process which can become very discouraging to the student. He needs to have a way to keep track of his own progress, a chance to see his own improvement. This can be accomplished in several ways. He can assess his improvement in specific areas of coordination, such as strength or endurance, by choosing several exercises which require that factor to be measured and recording the number of these exercises that he is capable of doing—at the start of the program and then again at two week intervals. As the amount of time spent in the training program increases so should his capacity for exercise. We can also measure improvement by recording the time in which he can cover a specific circuit of exercises or an obstacle course. As his coordination increases the speed in which he covers an obstacle course will decrease, not only because he will be able to move faster but also because his movements will be more efficient.

Another means of evaluation centers around the learning of specific activity skills. As previously suggested, the student should choose activities that he would like to become more proficient in. As he learns skills necessary for participation in these activities they can be checked off as an accomplishment. There are several audio-visual aids which can be particularily useful in this endeavor. Students can view loop films to see how a skill is performed, and through the aid of cinematography they can view their own performance in comparison. The uncoordinated student usually has not developed his sense of kinesthesis to the point where he can feel his own awkward movements, nor is he able to profit from verbal direction on how a movement should be done. By filming his activities he can look at and evaluate his own movements. Being able to see himself improve should benefit not only his self-image but also his understanding of the activities themselves.

No matter what the method used for evaluation, some effort should be made to keep a written record of what is taking place. It can provide a basis for evaluation of the program itself as well as the progress of the individual student.

The chart in Fig. 14-1 is designed so that the student himself can fill it out and the teacher can refer to it later. Enter the date in the space provided. List the specific exercises, stunts, and sports skills to be evaluated in the spaces provided in each section. After the testing, enter the number of repetitions done for each exercise, the time for the circuit or obstacle course, and check off the stunt activities and sports skills that have been learned. By using the same card for several trials it will be possible to compare past performance with present achievement.

It should be noted that when considering evaluation no mention has been made of comparing an individual's performance with any national norms or group averages. Though sometimes it is advantageous to know how a person stands in relation to the rest of a larger population, the uncoordinated student is already below the average and he usually knows it. Why emphasize the fact? Rather, concentrate the emphasis on how the person progresses in relation to his own past performance. How *he* can

Individual Activity Record

| Name: | | First Trial | Second Trial | Third Trial | Fourth Trial |
|---|---|---|---|---|---|
| | | Class: | | | |
| Activities | | (date) | (date) | (date) | (date) |
| Exercises | _____ <br> _____ <br> _____ <br> _____ <br> _____ | | | | |
| Circuit or Obstacle Course | | | | | |
| Stunt Activities | _____ <br> _____ <br> _____ <br> _____ | | | | |
| Sports Skills | _____ <br> _____ <br> _____ <br> _____ | | | | |

**Fig. 14-1**

improve is the important factor. Compare him with himself rather than with others—it is his improvement that counts. If more specific data is needed on pupil progress it is suggested that each student undergo formal testing upon entrance to the program (refer to Chapter 1), and at six month intervals.

# GLOSSARY OF TERMS AND POSITIONS

*Alignment*—a condition of body positioning in which, if standing, the head, shoulders, hips, knees and feet are all on the same line of axis which passes through the center of gravity and is perpendicular to the base of support. If seated, the body is aligned down through the hips to the base of support. See Fig. G-1.

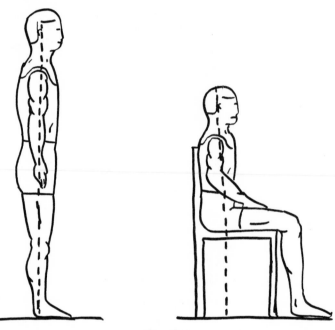

**Fig. G-1**

*Back lying*—a body position in which the person is lying on his back on the floor. The legs should be straight and together and the toes should be pointed. Unless otherwise stated the arms should be extended on the floor next to the sides of the body. The back of the head is on the floor with the focus on the ceiling. See Fig. G-2.

*Erect*—a position in which the alignment of the body places it in a perpendicular relationship to the floor with the head being the uppermost part. See Fig. G-3.

*Forward/backward stride*—the same position as the straddle stand except the legs are separated so that one is in front of the body and the other is behind it. The rest of the alignment is the same. See Fig. G-4.

**Fig. G-2**

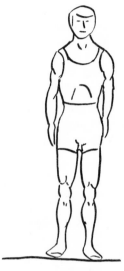

**Fig. G-3**

**Fig. G-4**

*Front lying*—lying with the stomach on the floor, legs straight and together with the toes pointed. The arms are bent with the hands on the floor in front of the face allowing the chin to rest on the backs of the hands. See Fig. G-5.

**Fig. G-5**

*Front support*—from a front lying position the hands are placed with the palms on the floor directly under the shoulders. Then the arms are straightened lifting the upper body off the floor. The body should remain in an aligned position. See Fig. G-6.

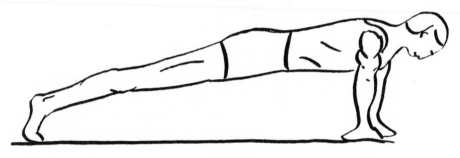

**Fig. G-6**

*Hurdle sit*—a sitting position in which one leg is flexed at the hip and knee allowing the lower leg to lie on the floor parallel to the front of the body, and the other leg flexed at the hip and knee placing the lower leg on the floor and the foot behind the seat. The leg in front is turned out at the hip and the back leg is turned in. Both knees should touch the floor. See Fig. G-7.

*Indian sit*—a sitting position with the legs flexed at the hip and knee, turned out at the hips and crossed at the ankles. The feet should be comfortably close to the body. The arms should rest easily on the knees. See Fig. G-8.

*Long sit*—a sitting position in which the legs are together and extended directly in front of the body. The toes should be pointed. The body should be aligned over the hips and the hands can rest comfortably on the thighs. See Fig. G-9.

**Fig. G-7**

**Fig. G-8**

**Fig. G-9**

*Lunge*—from a straddle stand the weight is shifted onto either the forward leg, if it is from a forward/backward stride, or to either leg if it was from a side straddle. The leg supporting the weight should bend at the knee and the trunk inclines over that leg from the hips. The arms should hang at the sides. See Figure G-10.

**Fig. G-10**

*Parallel position*—standing with the feet parallel to each other. See Fig. G-11.

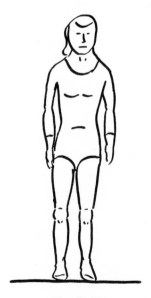

**Fig. G-11**

*Pike*—a position of the legs and trunk in which the legs, which are kept straight with the toes pointed, are brought as close to the chest as possible through flexion of the hips. See Fig. G-12.

**Fig. G-12**

*Side lying*—a reclining position with the weight on one hip and the side of the body. The legs are extended, one on top of the other with the toes pointed. One arm is extended along the floor beyond the head in line with the rest of the body. The top arm is bent in front of the body with the palm placed flat on the floor in front of the chest to aid in balance. See Fig. G-13.

**Fig. G-13**

*Squat*—from either a standing position or a straddle stand, the knees and hips are flexed allowing the body to lower. The heels may or may not leave the floor, depending on how deep into the squat the person bends. See Fig. G-14.

*Standing position*—a position of erect alignment, with the feet in parallel position, and the arms hanging losely at the sides. See Fig. G-15.

*Straddle sit*—very similar to the long sit except that the legs are spread wide apart. See Fig. G-16.

*Straddle stand*—a position of erect alignment, with the feet in parallel position and spread shoulder width apart. See Fig. G-17.

**Fig. G-14**

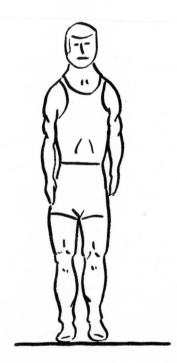

**Fig. G-15**

**Fig. G-16**

**Fig. G-17**

**Fig. G-18**

**Fig. G-19**

*Tuck*—a position of the legs and trunk in which the legs are flexed at the knees
   and hips and with the toes pointed. The knees are brought as close to the
   chest as possible. See Fig. G-18.
*Turn out*—a position of the legs and feet. Through external rotation at the hip the
   feet are placed with the heels together and the toes apart from each other.
   See Fig. G-19.

# GENERAL INDEX

# STUNT AND EXERCISE INDEX